A Long Way Home

One POW's story of escape and
evasion during World War II

A Long Way Home

One POW's story of escape and
evasion during World War II

BIG SKY PUBLISHING

Charles Granquist

First published in 2010

Big Sky Publishing Pty Ltd
PO Box 303
Newport, NSW
Australia
Phone: (61 2) 9918 2168
Fax: (61 2) 9918 2396
Email: info@bigskypublishing.com.au
Web: www.bigskypublishing.com.au

National Library of Australia Cataloguing-in-Publication entry

Author:	Granquist, Charles.
Title:	A Long Way Home : one POW's story of escape and evasion during World War II / Charles Granquist.
ISBN:	9780980658224 (pbk.)
Subjects:	Granquist, Charles.
	Prisoners of war--Greece--Biography.
	Prisoners of war--Australia--Biography.
	Prisoner-of-war escapes--Greece.
	World War, 1939-1945--Greece.
	World War, 1939-1945--Personal narratives.
Dewey Number: 940.5472495092	

Senior editor: Alistair Mival
Proof Reading and Edit: Diane Evans and Virginia Laugesen
Cover and Typesetting: Think Productions
Printed: by Ligare Pty Ltd

Cover Photo: On 30 March 1941 the author was on leave in Alexandria under 12 hours notice to sail for Greece. He visited an Egyptian photographic studio, had his photo taken, paid him in advance and asked that two copies be sent to his mother with no great confidence that she would get them. She did.

To my dear wife, Wendy, who nurtured and encouraged me through the long gestation period of this book, and my daughter, Sandra Stark, who was always there.

To my old mates, Jack "Lofty" Barker and Russell "Rusty" McWilliam, for the use of their memories, and to those members of my battalion, past and present, whose experiences I have taken from 'White Over Green', the history of the 2/4th Battalion.

I am also truly grateful to Jan Austen who transformed my poorly typed effort into a true manuscript.

CONTENTS

CHAPTER 1
THE EARLY DAYS

This is the story of an Australian boy who spent six years of his life away from his home during World War II. His story begins at Blaxland in the Blue Mountains. Born in 1922, I was brought home to a tent where I spent the first four years of my life. That tent with the sides rolled up features among some of my earliest memories.

My father, Charles, had returned from the First World War with a leg that had been badly wounded in France in 1917. A Soldiers Settlement grant of 52 acres in Rusden Road, Blaxland, allowed him to set about single-handedly building a poultry farm. Dad always had a streak of adventure in him. He was born in Sweden in a place called Karlskrona and ran away to sea at the age of 13 to become a cabin boy on a sailing ship. Most of his sailing was done on windjammers transporting wool and wheat.

What would possess a boy to leave his home at such a young age? I remember him once telling me that life in Sweden at that time was almost unbearable. Food was scarce and he had no desire to stay and starve. From what I understand he spent most of his twenties and thirties traversing the globe, often in horrendous weather, before finally settling in Australia.

He never returned to Sweden and was naturalised in 1913. He had visited many different countries but thought Australia was the only one worth living in. He clearly also felt it was worth fighting for and a year after war broke out in Europe he joined up. But for some strange reason he joined the AIF in 1915 and not the Navy. I don't know exactly why but I reckon it had a lot to do with a mate or two.

After the farm was up and running, my father – who everyone called 'Bob' – bought a ready-cut home from George Hudson which was delivered to Blaxland on a train. We had a big Clydesdale mare called 'Kitten' and a dray. Dad and Kitten made numerous two-mile trips to the railway station to bring all the materials to the farm.

It was only a one-bedroom home and when my sister Mary joined us (she had been living with my Aunty in Paddington) we both had to sleep on the partly enclosed verandah. A second bedroom was added later and my sister and I moved in there.

It wasn't just my father who had the urge to travel. My mother, Charlotte, who everyone called Lottie, was born in the north of England. She headed to Australia with her sister, stopping first in Perth before ending up in Sydney where she met Dad. She had never been on a farm in her life, but she had no alternative but learn to be a farmer's wife, which she appeared to do with good grace. She had to learn quickly because my father was forced to visit Randwick Military Hospital every year by complications with his wounded leg. At one stage the doctors wanted to amputate but he wouldn't have any of that because he feared it would end his farming. He was a very tough man.

I started school at Blaxland Primary School when I was five. It was two-and-a-half miles from the farm and each day I walked there with my sister. Blaxland was a very small school with about 12 pupils. The teacher was Mr Bill Worth and looking back I think he probably taught us well.

Bill's two great loves were cricket and gardening. In the park opposite the school was a concrete cricket pitch. On one side was the railway line and on the other was the Great Western Highway. Bill taught us to play a straight bat to any ball on the wicket but to hit anything off the wicket as hard as possible. He fostered in me a love for cricket and although only a very average player it has given me much pleasure all my life. I didn't, however, inherit the same love of gardening.

Old Bill was a very good cricketer, having played for NSW Colts in his younger days and he was a good coach. At the far end of the park was a German machine gun mounted on a concrete plinth with the usual inscription, "To our Glorious Dead", or something like that. It was, I believe, erected in honour of a local man, Harold Campbell, who had died of wounds he suffered fighting in Europe in 1916. We used to gather at this Memorial on Anzac Day, Armistice Day and, I think, Empire Day; when we sang the Recessional and other similar hymns designed to stir patriotism in our hearts.

This was the time of the Great Depression and there were many swagmen on the road going out west looking for work for there was none in the city. Many "swaggies" had a kelpie or blue heeler dog and their trademark was a billycan hanging from their swags. If old Bill saw one passing through, he would bring him in to the school for a mug of tea, which the swaggie drank sitting against the school wall in the shade. There was always a bowl of water for the dog.

The Depression days were grim, although as a young boy it didn't concern me too much. I do remember one Christmas when there were no presents. Fortunately, the bush around us was alive with wild flowers and my sister and I used to pick Waratahs and Christmas bush to brighten our home for the festive season.

My father, who had very little bush knowledge, employed a water diviner to pick out a spot for a well. He found one close to the house. Dad sank a well and sure enough there was water. Although it was wonderful to have a good source of water all the time, it brought snakes by the dozen. We lived with snakes around the house, snakes under the house and snakes in the house. One even found its way into Mum's clothes basket. One day our cat bailed up one outside. The snake was weaving its head from side to side as the cat, with intense concentration, followed every movement. Dad went inside and got the shotgun and blew the snake's head off. Not surprisingly, a shotgun going off right next to the cat's ear sent it straight up in the air in fright. He came down running and we didn't see him for days.

My father employed a chap called Gordon Hutchison for five shillings a week plus his keep. He lived in an old shack on the property. When the Depression really bit, Dad could not pay Gordon any more but allowed him to stay on in the hut. I remember Gordon getting a weekly dole coupon for five shillings worth of groceries and a packet of tobacco and papers. He had to walk seven miles to Penrith to get his coupon and buy his groceries and then carry them all the way back. He was a very capable young man who was badly affected by the Depression. His situation wasn't unique. When the economy finally picked up he got a job with a large tourist bus company and later became manager.

About half a mile from our place was a property, little better than a shack, which was owned by quite an important employee of the Sydney City Council. He spent weekends and holidays there with an Aboriginal woman called Daisy. During the week Daisy got very bored and often came over to our place and had a meal with us. I suppose it was unusual at that time when race relations were not what they are today. I think my parents' varied experiences and backgrounds meant they were more accepting than some. Sometimes Daisy went "walkabout" and would be gone for weeks but she always came back. She was a friendly, kind soul and I liked her.

Running a farm in the 1930s was a constant battle and one year we were in the path of a very bad bushfire. Dad, bad leg and all, had to fight hard to save the farm. He could not leave the fire and my mother sent me off to find him with a billy of tea. It was getting dark but I eventually found him. On the way back I got lost because there were burning tree stumps everywhere and it was hard to pick out the lights of the house. Eventually I made it home and it was a great relief after a big fright for a child who wasn't much older than about eight. The trees used to be home to many koalas but the fire wiped them out. To my knowledge they never came back.

It was about this time we were given a pony called Queenie because its original owner could not afford to feed her. She was a lovely, quiet horse on which I learnt to ride. We had a sulky, which made the trip to Blaxland much quicker. When I rode Queenie into Blaxland I had to keep at her all the way, but on the way back I could almost go to sleep as she cantered along.

I can only remember being very sick once as a boy. The illness was "scarletina", which is now more commonly known as scarlet fever. Seeing the doctor was quite a challenge. Dr Barrow was in Penrith and this involved Dad using the pony and sulky to go into Blaxland to ring him. Dr Barrow caught the train to Blaxland and Dad had to take him out to the farm before taking him back to the station. It was about this time my father got a Chevrolet truck. It had a fearful wheel wobble and was broken down almost as often as it was running. It could, however, carry a bigger load than the horse and dray and could do the trip to Blaxland a lot quicker.

There were times during the depression that we were stony broke. I remember Mum once saying to Dad: "Bob, we've got no money in the bank." Eggs were only a tuppence a dozen so they were never going to make Dad a fortune. Thankfully we were on a farm so we had food and never went hungry.

While times were tough I think we learnt to enjoy the simple pleasures in life. In January Mum would sometimes take Mary and me to Manly for a week. I loved going over in the ferry, especially when there was a heavy swell coming through Sydney Heads and the spray wet the decks. Mum would park us on the suitcases and head off to find a room; not far from the beach we hoped. The room would accommodate the three of us and there was invariably a gas-ring in the corner, although fish and chips were a big part of our holiday diet. I thought Manly was a magic place and still do, despite my holiday often comprising of only about two days on the beach and the remainder with bad sunburn.

After finishing primary school I went to Penrith Intermediate High at age about 11. Now I had to ride my bike two miles to Blaxland station, take the train to Penrith and walk a good mile to school before heading home the same way at the end of the day. To see my friends at weekends, or during the holidays, meant walking or riding to Blaxland and back. This, combined with a rather basic diet, kept me in good nick.

I was a slightly above average student and played cricket and rugby league in the seconds. We usually played Richmond or Katoomba as part of a three-team competition. On one occasion I played with the First XI on Richmond Oval. I don't think I did anything notable but I was happy just to play on an oval with a grandstand.

Boys of that age generally don't have much appreciation of beauty. However, there was one moment that has always stuck in my mind. I was riding my bike to the station about 7.00am one winter morning. It was a very cold but clear morning after a heavy frost. On the side of the road among some low scrub, the frost had settled on a myriad spider webs. As the rising sun shone on them it looked like a million diamonds. That thing of great beauty has stayed with me, an example perhaps – like the Manly ferry and fish and chips – that my boyhood, with its simple pleasures, was indeed a happy one. I had two wonderful parents and felt quite secure. The Blue Mountains were a great place to grow up. Blaxland village had grown and I had quite a few friends. Holidays and weekends were spent playing cricket and tennis or swimming in our pool in Florabella creek. I joined the Boy Scouts and went camping at various bush locations. My friend Bob and I used to paddle his canoe from Emu Plains, up the Nepean River, past where the Warragamba Dam is sited today, to Bents Basin where we would camp.

Meanwhile, my father, who hadn't known the difference between a cricket bat and a shovel, also developed a passion for cricket to rival my own. These were the glory days of Tests between England and Australia and I would often ride my bike to Blaxland to get a newspaper to keep up with the scores. Cricket was front page news in those Depression days and the names of Bradman, Woodfull, McCabe and Grimmett were household names then as are Ponting, Gilchrist, Waugh and Warne today. One day Dad bought a one-valve radio which required a dry battery and a wet one. Now we could follow the cricket on the radio. The best nights were when the Australians toured England and we could listen to the broadcast together. I could listen to Australian Tests when I was at home, but Dad was too busy working. The only drawback was the wet battery did not last long and Dad would have to harness up the pony and sulky and take it into the local service station/store which would lend him one while ours was being charged.

Dad was proud of his poultry farm, particularly the day it was inspected by a Mr Hadlington, from the Department of Agriculture, who gave it top marks. When I was 12 I was sent to learn chicken-sexing on a Saturday from a Mr Evans at Dundas, about 30 miles away. The ideal accuracy was 98% but I could only achieve 95%, which was good enough to sex our day-old chickens and those on nearby farm.

It was about this time that my family life changed forever. My father, who had endured so much, suffered a massive stroke that left him badly paralysed and unable to speak coherently. Gordon had left by then, but Mum was able to employ a young English migrant, whose name I can't remember, for five shillings a week and his keep and between the three of us we were able to keep the farm running.

My father died in my last term at school, just before the Intermediate Certificate. Tragically for the last few years of his life he was little better than a vegetable; his final days spent in the hospital that was part of the Lidcombe Old Men's Home.

Going to this place of last resort was always feared and it was said that the gates only opened one way, but we had no money for anything else.

It was tough few years. I visited him a number of times but was always saddened by the experience. The proud man who had boldly struck out from Sweden at just 13, fought for his adopted country, and built his farm despite a debilitating war wound was now almost a skeleton. What made it harder was he could no longer talk and I was just getting to know him when had his first stroke. In many ways his passing was a relief. He was 64. I was 14.

In later years I have come to realise that this kind, honest, hardworking man had taught me some basic principles of life that never left me. He always used to say: "one hand for the ship and one for yourself".

My Intermediate pass was two As and five Bs from seven subjects. Dad had always wanted me to go to the Royal Australian Naval College or Duntroon and my pass was good enough to sit the entrance exam. However, there were very few vacancies and it was necessary for me to get a job as soon as possible. Most of the jobs available were assembling radios at AWA or with Fleets Messengers. A family friend arranged an interview with Legacy and I was sent to Major Bros., a well-known paint manufacturing firm in those days. The Director was a returned serviceman who had lost an arm in France. There were a lot of other applicants but he took a shine to me and at 14 I started work. My first job was as a messenger boy with other duties. My pay was five shillings per week. The hours were nine to five weekdays and nine to noon on Saturday.

The steam train running down the Blue Mountains was called "The Fish" and I had to catch that at 7.30am. It arrived at Central Station at 8.40 am which meant I had to sprint across to the electric train to get to Wynyard and then another sprint across Wynyard Park to Australia House in Carrington Street where the office was. It was a reverse sprint at 5.00pm because The Fish left at 5.20pm. If I missed it I had to wait for the next one at 7.30pm and then, of course, there remained the two-mile walk home.

In 1938 my mother sold the farm, which was a stroke of good fortune because nobody wanted to buy poultry farms in those days. It was a deal with little cash attached to it but we got a weatherboard house in Blaxland village, white ants and all, as part of the deal. It really was a good move because it took all the pressure of running the farm off my mother and I now had a short walk to the station. Things were starting to look up. I had a good job, my wages had increased to eight shillings a week and I had a girlfriend called Marjory. My mother had a war widow's pension and, with what I was able to give her, we managed quite well.

I decided I needed to learn to dance as this seemed a very desirable thing for young men like me to do. Lessons were being held at the local Scout Hall so I went along to learn. The first lesson involved the waltz. The teacher was a large lady in a black dress with a spectacular red rose on her breast. As she whirled me round and round, all I could do was fix my eyes on that rose and hang on desperately. When this agony was over I rushed outside and was violently ill. So ended my dancing career. Even now I can't turn round twice without feeling giddy.

Despite my lack of dance skills, Marjory and I had some good times together. We went to the pictures once a week, normally on a Saturday afternoon. It was sixpence for the front stalls but ninepence for the back. I wanted to impress, so it had to be the back stalls for us. With a packet of Columbines for sixpence, it came to two shillings all up. When the opportunity presented itself we went in for some teenage experimentation, which led to nothing conclusive, but the promise of things to come – which never did.

In mid-1938 my mother let the home in Blaxland and we moved to a flat in Burwood. I enlisted in the Militia – 30th Battalion (NSW Scottish Regiment) – and this began my interest in all things military. I took my holidays to go to camp and thoroughly enjoyed the life.

With the outbreak of war in 1939 my mother decided to go back to Blaxland for the duration. I decided to join the A.I.F. and put my age up from 17 to 19 to do so. Like a lot of blokes at the time, I felt a sense of adventure despite seeing what war could do to a man like my father. At 19 you still had to have parental permission and I pressured my mother to sign. Afterwards I felt very sorry for the anguish I caused her. She didn't want to sign because she had seen how Dad had been badly knocked about and no doubt she held grave fears for her only son. She did not tell me not to go, but I knew she wasn't happy about it. I was a bit nervous someone might put me in and my real age would be discovered. I knew mum wouldn't, but I was not so sure about my sister, Mary.

Even so I was knocked back at my first attempt to enlist because of bad tonsils.

Mary was by now a nurse at Penrith Hospital so I immediately went to see her and arranged for my tonsils to be removed. When I was better I headed straight back to the Recruiting Depot at Moore Park where I was duly sworn in and posted to the 2/4th Battalion at Ingleburn. My father had been in the 4th Pioneer Battalion and our next-door weekend neighbour, Bon Tomkins, had been in the 4th Battalion in World War I where he lost his right arm. When I was all kitted out in my service uniform with the white over green patches on my shoulders I went to see Bon where he worked at Customs House. He was so overjoyed to see me in his old battalion colours you would have thought it was the second coming. He regaled me at great length with tales of the capture of Pozieres after months of heavy fighting and how they beat the Prussian Guards at Le Barque. I went back to camp feeling like a Greek god.

I had signals experience in the Militia so was posted to the Signal Platoon. Most of the men in my platoon came from the North West, but the battalion was heavily populated with men from the South West – Cootamundra, Junee, Wagga Wagga and other towns in that area. A few, like me, were from Sydney. There were snide remarks in some quarters that those enlisting in the A.I.F. did so because they were unemployed or wanted to escape from their wives. There were about 35 men in our platoon and I knew of none who were unemployed and only two who were married.

Early in January 1940 the battalion marched through Sydney with the 16th Brigade. It was a very hot day but the reception was stirring. On the 9th of January we handed in our palliases (a type of mattress), blankets and other gear. At 5.00am the next day we marched to Ingleburn Station where we boarded a troop train. The move was supposed to be secret but the railway line was a mass of people waving us goodbye and holding aloft banners wishing us good luck. The train went directly to Darling Harbour and stopped very close to our ship. We filed up the gangplank of the *Strathnaver*, a former P&O passenger ship requisitioned by the government for use as a troop ship. There were crowds of people everywhere – in launches, ferries and small boats. The singing was almost constant – "The Maori Farewell", "Wish Me Luck as You Wave me Goodbye", "Hang out the Washing on The Siegfried Line", etc.

Just after lunch we sailed through The Heads. This was a part of Sydney that meant a lot to me when I was a child. But this was not a holiday. On this day the 2/4th Battalion was heading off to its war. And it would be nearly six years before I saw Sydney again.

CHAPTER 2
TO PALESTINE

Just outside Sydney Heads we were joined by six ships carrying the New Zealand contingent and the warships that were to escort us on the first part of our voyage. The battleship *HMS Ramillies* and two Australian cruisers, *HMAS Australia* and *HMAS Canberra*, were an impressive and comforting sight. The *Strathnaver* had not been fully converted to a troop ship and still carried a full complement of stewards and stewardesses. I shared a cabin with Ben Connor, an old schoolmate of mine from Blaxland. All we had to do was sweep out our cabin and leave any rubbish outside the door.

Having my tonsils removed had prevented me from joining my battalion until after Christmas and I had missed most of the training at Ingleburn. Thankfully, my militia experience had prepared me well. The first day out, work began on weapons and signals training as well as guard duty at posts all over the ship. In spite of all that the trip early on felt more like a holiday cruise than a troop ship voyage. And the food was also good – much better than Ingleburn.

I felt some apprehension about joining this group of men for the first time, especially when most of them were 10 years older than me. Fortunately, I was quickly accepted and some long-lasting mateship sprung up with a number of these good men, cemented by some happy times at night in the canteen. Remember, I was supposed to be 19. At last I felt free from the fear that someone might report me for being underage. It was a feeling I'd carried with me since the moment I saw a furious mother marching her underage son out of the Ingleburn camp to the amusement of hundreds of men.

The weather was fine and warm all the way down the east coast and it made our large convoy with its warship escorts a spectacle to behold. It wasn't long before we were sailing far south in the Great Australian Bight to avoid surface raiders and submarines. The swell increased and a fair number of men were troubled by sea sickness. Fortunately, I was not one of them, although I did go a bit green. Our first port of call was Fremantle and it was quite exciting to experience the ship berth. I had never been out of New South Wales; not even that far out of Blaxland. Perth might well have been at the other end of the world as far as I was concerned.

We were given leave until midnight and promptly joined the mass of Australian and New Zealand soldiers who had invaded Perth along with sailors from Britain, France and Australia. A group of us ended up in a hotel on a hill overlooking the Swan River with a Perth-based brother of a member of our platoon. The following afternoon we sailed out of Fremantle and into the Indian Ocean where the convoy re-assembled. This was our last look at the Australian coastline. Our big adventure was unfolding before our eyes. Until then we had thought we were going to England to prepare to fight in France, where the Allied armies were facing the German threat. Instead, we learned we were going to Palestine. Later that afternoon the Australian cruisers left us, sailing through the convoy flying the signals "Good-bye and Good Luck". From that point our escorts were warships of the Royal Navy.

The daily grind of training, guard duty and fatigues was monotonous but at least it was broken at night by some very good stage shows. Boxing was popular and there were some very good contests enjoyed by a big audience. On the morning of Australia Day, January 26, a ceremony was held that ended with the *Ramillies* firing a salute. The rest of the day was declared a holiday which went down well with all of us.

A few days later we sighted Colombo. A huge sign – "CEYLON FOR GOOD TEA" – left us in no doubt where we were. Most of us had never seen another country, so we were buzzing with excitement after being given shore leave for the afternoon. We had very little money so spent most of our time roaming Colombo and doing a little bargaining with the locals. Some of our boys, who had been on the arak, an alcoholic drink distilled from the juice of palm trees, decided to take a ride in and on top of a tram. The tram ride came to a swift halt when forced to stop by a large white bull on the line. Despite all the yelling and abuse directed its way, the bull refused to move so a couple of the boys got off the tram and planted their military boots right on its backside. The bull galloped off at great speed but the locals were not at all pleased because they considered such animals to be sacred. Our boys beat a hasty retreat before they could cause any more offence.

The following day we sailed out of Colombo. The next night we glimpsed the North Star and realised we had crossed the equator into the northern hemisphere. I remember it well because we were soon joined by a British aircraft carrier, a vessel none of us had ever seen before. The day after the carrier arrived, a plane crashed from its deck into the sea during an exercise. One of our escorts quickly dispatched a boat to make a successful rescue.

As we sailed on our training was stepped up. Weapons and target practice became more intense, along with boat drills and action stations. We were also given a series of lectures on Palestine and its people, and how we were to behave towards them. Our next sighting of land turned out to be the barren rocks of Aden which, to be honest, failed to impress. However, attitudes quickly changed after we were given leave to go ashore and found many bazaars and shops filled with cheap but interesting wares. I bought a pair of white silk pyjamas with three red lions emblazoned across the front. I still don't quite know why a boy from Blaxland felt the need for such night attire and they certainly did not fit the lifestyle of an Australian infantryman on his way to war. There was no end of rude remarks from my mates. Nevertheless, I continued to wear the pyjamas – even after the first wash which caused red dye to run all over the white silk!

Our one day in Aden was marked by rain, the first the region had seen in two and a half years. After leaving port the convoy separated and the *Strathnaver* pushed on with three other ships without escort at fair speed. In a message to all troops the Commanding Officer, Lieutenant Colonel P. A. Parsons, had this to say, and I quote the 2/4th Battalion history:

"We are now nearing the end of our cruise and should soon commence our new life in Palestine: the land which gave us Christianity and Judaism and which has been the object of pilgrimage for devout Christians, Jews and Moslems down the centuries. To this Holy Land men, in olden days, would undergo the most horrible hardships to visit. It is a land which has been properly described as the most interesting country in the world; but a land so small that it is easy to motor from north to south in a single day, or from east to west in one morning".

He went on to describe the main features of the country, the climate, the ancient conflict between the Arabs and the Jews, the currency and the importance of security on account of the activity of enemy agents in the country. He concluded:

"Let me take this opportunity of thanking all ranks for the great camaraderie which exists on this troop ship and for the discipline shown throughout the voyage. I am sure that associations formed on this ship will be everlasting and will greatly assist my unit in carrying out the difficult tasks they may have to face in the future".

We reached the Suez just before midnight and left again early in the morning, heading through the Bitter Lakes and past a World War I memorial. It was very late at night we at last reached our destination, El Kantara. The place was a hive of activity under a glare of artificial light and we disembarked even though it was midnight. The movement officer was a very dapper British captain.

"The Sergeant will tell you where to go and what to do," he barked at the rough and ready Aussies.

From somewhere down the back, a loud voice called out: "Fuck the Sergeant".

The Captain responded in a very cultured tone: "You hold him and I'll fuck him".

He had no trouble with the troops after that.

The British Army looked after us very well with a hot meal and a cut lunch for the following day. They also issued each of us with a camel hair blanket which was most welcome on such a cold night. Early in the morning we squeezed ourselves and our gear into a troop train and set off for Palestine. At the first sign of daylight the men began to stir and the race was on to be the first to use the only toilet. This wasn't at all easy as the aisle was full of equipment and sleeping men. Not surprisingly, curses rang out around the carriage as soldiers were woken from their slumber by a misplaced boot on their hand or another part of their anatomy. Eventually we settled down and began to pay more attention to this strange land we were travelling through. We were in the Sinai Desert – a barren, featureless expanse of, well, nothing. Every now and then we spotted a collection of crude tent dwellings which, we were told, were occupied by Bedouins. I'd like to say something more caught my eye but there really was nothing else. All the same, it was a bit of an eye-opener for someone who had not even seen outback Australia. Our family could not afford to travel when I was growing up. I had never clapped eyes on Brisbane or Melbourne but in just a few weeks I had crossed an ocean, been given a taste of foreign lands and now found myself passing through the Sinai – and all at government expense!

And so we sat and watched the desert roll by, gratefully wolfing down the cut lunches given to us at El Kantara and waiting patiently to get to wherever we were going.

Chapter 2 - To Palestine

CHAPTER 3
IN THE HOLY LAND

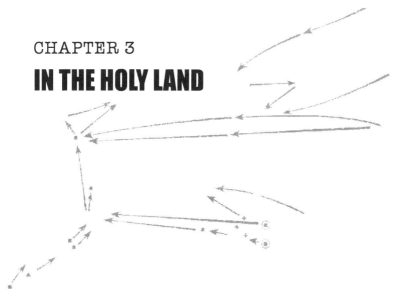

In this strange, barren and treeless land of Arabs, donkeys and camels, we were fostered by the 2nd Battalion of the Black Watch. Personally, it was terrific to see the Black Watch Tartan again because the 30th Battalion, which I had left to join the A.I.F., was affiliated with the regiment. They had been in Palestine for quite some time and readily taught us some of the tricks of dealing with the Arab vendors. When our battalion fought in Crete a year later, it did so alongside the same men.

But that was still some way off. Now we were more concerned with where we would sleep and it was heartening to find the Black Watch had erected our tents for us ready to move into in the camp at Julis, 15 miles north of Gaza. These tents had been made in Cawnpore (now Kanpur) in India, and as we found out later, it was very hard work to erect one. Each tent was big enough to fit 12 men on low stretchers. The ground was very rocky and we were quickly set to work clearing a company parade ground and getting the camp into shape. A few days after arriving we received our first pay in the local currency, piastres. We celebrated that night in the NAAFI, short for Navy, Army and Air Force Institutes, which ran canteens in the British Army.

It was here that I met a Methodist minister I knew from Blaxland. He spent some time telling me he was working hard to abolish the "wet" canteens. I never saw him again. Perhaps they took him away and shot him!

New weapons soon arrived – Bren guns to replace the Lewis machine guns, two-inch mortars, Boyes anti-tank rifles and, to the delight of the carrier platoon, new Bren carriers. Training was now on in earnest, with route marches to toughen us up for the company and battalion exercises, some of them at night. The Signal Platoon got stuck into mastering its job of providing vital communications. On one occasion we dug a full battalion trench system. It was hard work and in hindsight more related to World War I fighting than what we later experienced. We were gradually getting into good shape. In February Britain's Foreign Secretary Anthony Eden, later to become Prime Minister, and General Archibald Wavell, the commander of all Middle East forces, dropped in for a visit the day after we arrived in Palestine. General Wavell spoke to us about the current military situation and what he thought might happen in the future.

In March the rains came and turned the camp into a sea of mud which made life rather difficult. However, life brightened up considerably when we were granted leave to visit Tel Aviv and Jerusalem, about an hour away by bus. I was surprised to find Tel Aviv was a modern city with wide streets and what would be described as a Continental atmosphere. There was no such thing as six o'clock closing and you didn't even have to go to a pub for a drink. Every café and restaurant served liquor along with inexpensive, but excellent, food. As an added bonus you had no difficulty finding a cheap shampoo and hair cut, or a place to get your boots polished.

Tel Aviv boasted a wonderful beach. At one end was the wreckage of a ship that brought Jewish refugees escaping Hitler's persecution. The ship had been run ashore, allowing its passengers to scramble off and take flight in all directions to escape the clutches of the Palestine police.

Leave in Jerusalem was a different proposition. As a former Sunday school teacher my initial fascination was with the Old City. A good mate of mine, Gary Hart, was a great help. Although not particularly religious, he had read ancient Israeli history and knew all the places of interest. We visited the Wailing Wall and walked the Via Dolorosa which is traditionally considered the road that Jesus walked to his crucifixion. I marvelled at the Church of the Holy Sepulchre, the Hill of Golgotha and the Church of All Nations in the Garden of Gethsemane, where Australia had contributed some tiles for the floor. It was a haven of peace and quiet after the noise and terrible smells I encountered in other parts of the Old City.

On later visits to Jerusalem, five of us hired a car, the equivalent of a big Buick, and spent the day visiting sites outside the city. I have fond memories of enjoyable trips to the Sea of Galilee, Nazareth, Jericho, the Dead Sea and Bethlehem. These trips generally involved a boozy lunch before the driver delivered us back to Jerusalem and the bus. The drivers were always Arabs – very friendly and eager to please. The war seemed far away, especially during one particular four-day leave to Tel Aviv. We ate two big meals a day and drank plenty of strong local beer, which the troops called "Claws and Feathers". By the last day we had run out of money, so retired to the beach for some surfing and lying in the sun. These leave periods were wonderful, but we couldn't go often because we couldn't afford it!

In early May we moved to Qastina where it was our turn to do the hard work and get the camp ready for the 17th Victorian Brigade which was arriving from Australia. By now the temperature was scorching. The Khamsin, a dry hot wind, was blowing sandstorms across the desert from Persia (now Iraq and Iran). Around this time the 6th Division was re-organised and we were transferred to a new Brigade, the 19th, which comprised the 2/4th, 2/8th and 2/11th Battalions. The 2/8th came from Victoria and 2/ll th from Western Australia.

On the 10th of May the German "Blitzkrieg" began sweeping through Europe and in next to no time France was defeated. The bulk of the British Army escaped at Dunkirk and the Italians declared war on the Allies in early June. These were desperate days indeed as Britain, the Dominions and Greece now stood alone against powerful enemies. The main naval base in the Mediterranean was the Egyptian city of Alexandria. The anti-aircraft guns were manned by Egyptian gunners. When an Italian aircraft appeared over Alex the "Gyppos" decamped and were last seen disappearing in a cloud of dust over the sandhills. The British gunners manning the anti-aircraft defences in Haifa in Palestine were promptly dispatched to Alexandria. Our battalion was then combined with the 2/1st Field Artillery Regiment to form "X" and "Y" anti-aircraft regiments to man the Haifa guns. Under the guidance of British instructors, we quickly discovered the mysteries of range-finders, predictors and fuse setters. We were quartered in an old, unused hospital near the oil tank farm. Of course, it was the Italians' first target and sure enough they hit it. It burned for days. At night you could read a newspaper by the light of the fire.

After that we were moved to Mt Carmel which was a pleasant spot perched above the city. The guns were 3.7 inch A.A. and were very destructive to aircraft if you could lob a shell somewhere nearby. It wasn't long before the Italians returned for another go in late July. The Savoia 79s, flying at about 15,000 feet, dropped nearly 100 bombs. We got a few shots away but failed to score any hits. The planes did extensive damage to the city and surrounding residential areas, and many civilians were killed or wounded. Some of us were sent to help clear the damage and search the collapsed buildings for trapped people. I didn't find any survivors but helped to pull out some of those who had been killed. For many of us this was our first experience of violent death and the consequences of war.

Some trained Allied gunners soon arrived to man the guns and in early August we moved out to a spot near Acre, of Crusades fame, in what is now Northern Israel. Our camp was in an old poultry farm, which wasn't too bad apart from the smell. Someone had once planted a lot of eucalypts which made us Aussies feel very at home. There were no shower facilities so once a week we were sent by companies to the old Turkish baths in Acre to clean off the dust and grime. The baths dated back to well before Crusader times and the stone seats had quite pronounced hollows where backsides had sat for centuries. We were given quite a bit of day leave to Haifa which, like Tel Aviv, was modern and cosmopolitan.

In late August we moved from Acre to Kilo 89, a big camp just north of Gaza. Here we received a new commanding officer, Lt. Col. Ivan Dougherty who, at 33, was the youngest battalion Commander in the 6th Division. He proved to be a wonderful leader, admired by his troops, who accepted him as a man of fairness and great ability.

The powers-that-be seemed determined to keep us moving and it wasn't long before we were sent to a rest camp at Hadera where I had no duties to worry about except the rare kitchen fatigue. All we had to amuse ourselves was a good surf beach or the occasional day leave to Haifa. No wonder the day the A.I.F. staged a race meeting at Barbara, bookmakers and all, proved to be a great day out for everyone. However, all good things come to an end and we soon returned to Kilo 89 where intensive training again started in earnest. One battalion exercise took place out in the desert near Beersheba and close to some sulphur mines. The fierce desert heat and the smell of the sulphur made it seem as though you were in Hades.

Gary Hart and I were sent to Tel Rafa with a Marconi pack wireless set and a section of men to watch and report on aircraft activity. Getting across the Sinai to Tel Rafa involved travelling by truck to Khan Yunis before switching to camels after the road ended. The camels, led by an Arab bloke, were quite comfortable except when you had to get up and down. Gary and I settled into a small tent with our wireless set which appeared ancient but worked better than it looked. We communicated via Morse code and when operating on battery power could only receive messages. To transmit one of us had to wind a handle while the other used the Morse key. Unless there were enemy aircraft about all we had to do was make a routine report every hour. The rest of the time was ours. There was a wonderful beach about 50 yards away with excellent surf. One day a dolphin swam between my legs. Thinking it was a shark, I reached the beach in record time!

The Arab vendors turned up as usual bearing little trays of sweets, hot lemonade and other goodies. We gorged ourselves on the most delicious melons. It shouldn't have come as a surprise but we were soon on the move again, this time back to Kilo 89. Around September I got one stripe and was sent to the Infantry School of Signals at Nathanya for a six-week course. N.C.O.s from every infantry battalion in Palestine were there for a demanding but satisfying course. When it ended I was informed that the battalion had moved to Egypt where the 6th Division was assembling for the Western Desert campaign. I was issued with a rail warrant and caught the train to Cairo where I changed for Alexandria. There, a battalion truck picked me up and took me to the camp at Burg El Arab.

Our time in Palestine had turned us into a highly efficient infantry battalion. Morale was high, strong friendships had formed and we had seen a lot of an interesting country. We had thoroughly enjoyed ourselves. However, those almost peaceful days were soon to change.

CHAPTER 4
THE REAL THING

At Burg El Arab I moved back into my old tent. After six weeks away from my mates I was very pleased to see them all again. They had certainly looked after me. My surplus gear had come with them from Palestine and I had a stretcher and blankets ready for me to settle in straight away. The tents were all dug in to a depth of about three feet to give us some sort of protection from air raids. Before I got there a terrific storm had flooded the camp and filled the dug-outs, soaking blankets and gear. Lucky me! I was called up to the CO's office where he congratulated me on just missing out on a distinguished pass in my course. A slight weakness in the mysteries of electricity – which I still have – had brought me undone.

We were only 10 miles from Alexandria and it was immediately evident that we had entered a war zone. Almost every night brought an air raid and the sky was lit up by searchlights and exploding AA shells. The battalion was busy taking part in brigade and divisional manoeuvres in the desert area. It was hot and dusty work but right on cue the usual locals turned up, seemingly from nowhere, with dates, figs and warm soft drinks to sell. Back at camp at the end of the day the meagre shower facilities we just good enough to wash off the bulk of the dust and sweat. At least the food was pretty good. When we could afford it, usually on pay night, we would buy a case of beer. Victoria Bitter was most blokes' favourite – two dozen large bottles individually packed in straw in a wooden crate.

It was mid-December when things started to happen. We were ordered to fill our packs with two blankets, spare socks and underwear. Everyone was issued with three days' hard rations – bully beef and biscuits. Ammunition was distributed and we were put on six hours' notice to move. All personal gear, including my prized silk pyjamas, had to be packed in a kit bag which would be stored until our return.

We were still waiting as Christmas drew closer. A big mail consignment helped alleviate the boredom. It was wonderful to get several letters from my mother and Mary plus a large Christmas cake which the whole tent devoured in no time at all. Being on short notice to move, we had our Christmas early. The Khamsin was blowing on the day, making it cold, windy and dusty. Dinner was served in the traditional manner – roast goose with all the trimmings and plum pudding. A good helping of beer left everybody feeling full and happy. Christmas parcels containing tinned cake, dried fruit, cheese and other goodies from the Lord Mayor's Patriotic Fund were an added bonus. For some time we had been keyed up waiting for our move to the battle zone and it was good to have a relaxing day, free of tension.

After Christmas we learnt the British forces operating out of Mersa Matruh, located on the Mediterranean, had pushed the Italians back to Sidi Barrani, about 20km from the Libyan border, and then out of Egypt. Meanwhile, we were still packed and waiting. Finally, on the last day of 1940, a large convoy of New Zealand trucks arrived. We climbed on board and headed west. New Year's Day 1941 passed virtually unnoticed as we travelled 130 dusty miles west from Mersa Matruh to Sallum. Sometimes the going was smooth, other times it was rough and we bounced around on the hard floor of our three-ton truck.

We now knew why the wait at Burg El Arab had been so long. It was thought that Bardia might be abandoned by the Italian occupiers and General Wavell had ordered the 19th Brigade to stand by in case it was required to head there by sea to occupy the fortress. What a pity it didn't happen. It would have been a much more enjoyable trip than days spent thumping across the desert in a truck.

We travelled for three days, getting our first sight of a battlefield along the way. Burnt out and damaged trucks, guns and tanks littered the desert together with rifles and machine guns abandoned by a retreating army. We climbed Halfaya Pass to the top of the 600-foot high escarpment on the Egyptian-Libyan border that was strategically very important. At the top our CO got us off the trucks a bit earlier than he needed to. He was worried the trucks might kick up too much dust and create an aiming point for Italian artillery. We later realised there was so much dust it didn't matter. After three days we gladly took the opportunity to stretch our legs. There wasn't much to see except a few thorn-bushes and miles and miles of desert.

With the sound of the guns at Bardia ringing in our ears, we marched to our position just outside the fortress and took over the area previously occupied by a battalion from 16th Brigade which had moved up to the start line for the initial assault. It was the middle of the night and very cold. We had been issued with lambskin jerkins that were worn with the hide outside. Later we learnt the Italians believed they were bullet-proof vests.

The guns boomed away all night and then just before dawn an enormous barrage opened up – the first time we had ever heard such a thing. We were very close to our artillery positions and the Italian counter-battery fire started to fall around us. Fortunately, there were very few casualties. It was the first time I had been under fire and I was a little anxious. We took cover in what we called "sangars", which were constructed by digging down as far you could (not far in a stony desert) before building a circle of protective stones.

The initial attack in this sector brought immediate success and we soon observed long lines of prisoners moving to the rear. However, the Victorian 17th Brigade had encountered much stronger resistance in its attack from the south and there were still some Italian positions holding out. That night we moved to the sector with orders to advance through the breached wire and mop up the trouble spots.

As we came to the wire mid-morning I encountered my first dead Australian soldier. He was from one of the Victorian battalions and had been left hanging on the wire. An Englishman in our platoon, who had served in the Infantry in World War I and seen plenty of this (I think he was in his forties and put his age down to serve again), became a bit hysterical. The rest of us were very quiet. To leave one of our own on the wire as we moved on was difficult but we had a job to do. There was little opposition and by early afternoon we were on the heights overlooking the town and harbour and it was all over.

The next day we rested before piling into trucks the following night and heading west towards Tobruk, which was still held by the Italians, in Libya. It was a rough and slow trip; the road was broken up and jammed with trucks, tanks and artillery pieces. Our morning arrival was interrupted by shrapnel fire. The Italians were lobbing shells that exploded around 20-30 feet above us, an effective measure against troops in the open. It wasn't a very polite welcome to Tobruk, but it made us jump out quickly and get out of the area. Our platoon commander, Lt. Wally Capper, had been transferred to Quartermaster and our OC was now Sgt. Bernie O'Mara, a very fine soldier who had been with us since Ingleburn.

We were based on the eastern side of Tobruk with the sea on our right. A series of deep wadis, or gullies, ran down to the sea. Our position was in Wadi Belgassem and the signal platoon swiftly established a signal office and began the job of laying telephone cable to the forward companies. This was a slow job as the ground was very rough and was being swept by occasional bursts of Italian machine-gun fire.

When this job was finished we went back to our wadi and dug some two-man slit trenches in the forward slope. The Italians started to shell us regularly but these were landing on the reverse slope, so if you had time to jump into your slit trench you were relatively safe. However, for obvious reasons, the pioneers had dug the latrines some distance away towards the bottom of the reverse slope. This made a visit more interesting than it should have been. As soon as you heard the sound of the guns you made a hasty exit, and the whole exercise made for an excellent laxative.

We occupied this position for about 10 days under continuous shelling. One night I was on duty in the signal office when the line to one of the forward companies went dead. I presumed that it had been cut by shell fire and set out to locate and repair the break. As it was too dark to see, this was accomplished by running the cable through your hand until you found the break. Instead I found two signallers fast asleep at the end of the line. They had quite rightly turned down the volume on the phone buzzer for security reasons, but to go to sleep at your post is a very serious crime. Knowing how tired they were, I just woke them up and told them how lucky they were that the battalion had not been trying to get an important message through to their company. I was furious that I had been dragged out in the middle of the night to stumble across the stony desert for no good reason, but the matter stopped there. We were all very tired.

As the Italian artillery, which was very accurate, shelled us with monotonous regularity, the forward companies sent out patrols every night to probe the enemy defences and locate his strongpoints. These patrols often provoked a torrent of Italian fire. They were certainly not short of ammunition. After being relieved by the 2/5th Battalion, we pulled back some distance for a rest near the sea where we had our first wash for more than a fortnight. It was a welcome change after being allowed only one water bottle a day for drinking and washing. Clean shirts, underclothing and socks were issued and after a deep sleep we felt like new men.

It had been decided that the assault on Tobruk should be from the southern side and 19th Brigade would be playing a major part. A long night march, with no smoking, talking and generally as little noise as possible, got us to a position outside the southern perimeter of the garrison where we were ordered to lie "doggo" until nightfall and then to prepare for an attack the next morning, January 21. Unfortunately for Ron "Pop" Lilyman, a ration truck failed to see him having a snooze in a shallow slit trench and ran over him. He was evacuated to the Casualty Clearing Station and eventually made a full recovery. The initial assault was to be made by battalions of the 16th Brigade, who planned to breach the wire, capture and clear the enemy forward posts and then swing right and left.

When the 2/4th Battalion got through the breach the Italian artillery laid down a fierce barrage, including big shells from the cruiser San Georgio which had been sunk by air attack but had settled upright in shallow water and could still operate its guns. Our first objective, on a due north bearing, was an Italian sector headquarters at Sidi Mahmud. To reach it we had to cross the Bardia road which ran straight as a die with an Italian heavy machine-gun firing straight down it. Happily he was firing a bit high when we crossed. I could hear the bullets buzzing over our heads. Later he made a correction and some men following behind us were hit.

The Italian Headquarters surrendered and the occupants, including a priest, were moved off to the rear. One of our officers, a staunch Catholic, approached the CO to tell him the priest wanted to go back and get his rosary beads. The CO told him in no uncertain terms what the priest could do and that he should get on with the battle.

The forward companies now turned north-west with orders to capture the fortress headquarters which was just a couple of miles away. Fred Apthorp, Lloyd "Grumpy" Skelton and I started laying a signals line to them. It was hard-going and we were carrying a lot of heavy cable. Grumpy found a wheelbarrow in a dugout and we loaded it up with cable and laid the first half-mile.

We were bunched together, joining the cables together when we copped a salvo of shells. Fred and I went to ground but Grumpy took off, still pushing the wheelbarrow. By the time we got the cable laid to the forward company it had captured the fortress headquarters and our battalion headquarters had shifted as well, so all that work was wasted. We reeled in all that cable in and set about connecting the companies to the new battalion headquarters. There was no wireless because these were still early days and the army was living with World War I conditions.

The battle for Tobruk was virtually over and we could get a bit of sleep. Having been on the move for about 17 hours, we needed no rocking. In the morning our platoon was selected to lead the battalion into the town of Tobruk. We marched into the main square with that feeling of exuberance which, I have no doubt, has always been felt by the victors. We were soon to learn what the reverse side of the coin was like.

The Italian flag was hauled down and a very enterprising member of our platoon, Rusty McWilliam, grabbed an Australian slouch hat from the brigade signal truck (we were wearing tin helmets) and attached it to the rope. It was hoisted to the masthead and proudly flew over Tobruk's main square. We explored the town and were amazed by the opulence of some of the Italian officers' quarters. They must have had a very comfortable war before this Allied-led disaster struck them. We found a couple of very nice villas to bed down and made use of the baths and showers which were a wonderful luxury.

Brigadier Robertson, the officer commanding 19th Brigade, had said at a dinner before leaving Australia that he had captured a Turkish general in World War I and was planning to capture an admiral in this one. When it was pointed out that admirals were not normally found away from their battleships, he responded: "We'll see". On entering the town, Lieutenant Hennessy of the 6th Divisional Cavalry was approached by an Italian naval officer who explained that he had been sent to lead him to naval headquarters where an Italian admiral was waiting to surrender. When the admiral proffered his sword, Hennessy declined and sent for Brigadier Robertson. "Red Robbie" duly arrived and was directed to the room where Admiral Massimiliano Vietina explained that he and 1,500 of his men wished to surrender. The surrender was accepted and so Brigadier Robertson got his admiral and the 2/4th Battalion – and a troop of the 6th Divisional Cavalry – technically captured a battleship. The ship was the *San Giorgio*, the source of the big shells that gave us curry the morning before.

There was plenty of liquor and good tinned food for the taking and we lived the life of Riley until told that we would be moving out the next day. So much for the spoils to the victors! Our next destination was Gazala where later in the year Rommel decisively defeated the British armour.

CHAPTER 5

DERNA, BENGHAZI AND BACK

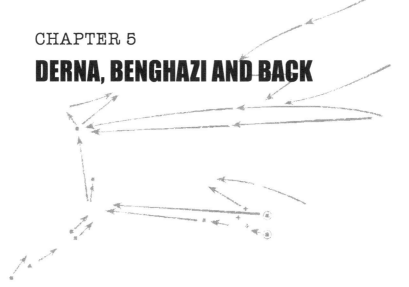

We were on the left flank of the 19th Brigade and our approach to Derna was across the usual stony, featureless desert where the only sign of growth was camel thornbush. The importance of digging in that night was reinforced the next morning when our position was strafed by enemy fighters. Unfortunately for Neville May, his slit trench wasn't enough to stop a large calibre bullet ploughing through his shoulder and ending his Libyan campaign.

The next morning the battalion moved forward to Wadi Derna. Nobody expected this to be an enormous ravine – deep, steep and very rough. It took almost all night for A and C Companies to get some men across the wadi where they immediately came under attack. The enemy was the most aggressive we had so far encountered. Signallers followed just behind advancing soldiers, laying cable as we went – a slithering, stumbling job. By the time we got across the wadi the companies had been reinforced and repulsed several determined attacks.

We connected the line to A Company before Keith "Killer" Turnbull, Tommy Fitzpatrick and I headed off to find C Company which had moved to the left to protect the exposed flank. Laying cable as we went, we were moving along the lip of the wadi when we stumbled upon a heavy machine gun post.

Thankfully the gun was pointing in the opposite direction and the three Italian soldiers manning it were so surprised they surrendered without resistance. I left Keith and Tommy and moved up the slope to see if I could locate C Company. When I reached to the top I was shocked to see at least a company of Italian soldiers spread out about 300 yards away and trotting towards me. Not being a rifleman I would have liked a bit more time to prepare myself. But time there wasn't and I got down behind a tree and fired my first shot in anger.

My nerves were jangling and my mouth almost painfully dry, but despite that my first shot hit the bloke in front and he went down behind a thornbush. I emptied my .303 magazine in a hurry and was feverishly trying to get a new clip out of my disorganised pouch when a Bren gun opened up to the right. Praise be, it stopped the Italians in their tracks. Taking advantage of the cover from the first trees we had seen in Libya, I beat it back to join the others. We threw the machine gun down the wadi and, using gestures, instructed the 'Itis' to cross the wadi and give themselves up on the other side. All troops on the western side of the wadi had been ordered not to waste resources by using soldiers to escort prisoners.

In the years that have followed that first taste of real action I have often thought about that first man I shot. I fervently hope that I only wounded him and that he one day got home to his family after the war ended. Perhaps he did, perhaps he didn't. I will never know. It doesn't matter how you think about it. When you strip away the gloss and the ritual, an infantry battalion is really only a killing machine and I was part of one.

We located C Company and connected them up. Both companies were now across the wadi in strength and, despite fierce opposition, were gradually pushing the enemy back and gaining a firm foothold on the western side. However, Division had received reports that a strong force was massing to the south on our exposed left flank and ordered the companies back across the wadi so that the whole battalion could be brought to bear on this threat. It was major disappointment to all those who had fought so hard to get a secure bridgehead, and the signallers who had to reel in all their cable – a much harder job than laying it. We were relieved by the 2/5th Battalion and moved down to the Mechili road but the enemy had scarpered. We pushed on down the escarpment to Derna. The town had been looted by the retreating Italians as they evacuated before the Arabs finished the job, but we managed to find some eggs and tinned food.

We slept in Derna that night and the next morning set out along the road to Giovanni Berta (now known as Al Qubah). We moved very gingerly because the road had been heavily mined. Although the engineers had been busy clearing a route there were only narrow lanes to follow. Near Giovanni Berta we were picked up by transport which ferried us to Barce. The countryside was quite different to the desert we had become used to; the green fields and white farmhouses were a delight to the eyes.

It was raining heavily and for the first time we had mud to contend with. Once the truck bogged and we had to get out and push. We were delayed for some time while the 2/11th Battalion dealt with an enemy rearguard but eventually we made it down the escarpment to Benina which was only a few miles from our final destination of Benghazi.

At a big Iti ordnance dump we loaded a big supply of tinned food into the platoon ute along with some beer – the first we had found in Libya. The following day the battalion waited while the formalities for the surrender of the city were concluded before moving in to carry out garrison duties. The bulk of the defeated Italian Army was in full retreat to the west and the 7th Armoured Division had cut across the desert and was fighting to destroy it at Beda Fomm, just south of Benghazi. Our battalion, minus the garrison company, was ordered to join the battle, but by the time we got there it was all over and the road and the surrounding desert was full of burning tanks and trucks.

The Italian Army in Libya had been comprehensively beaten. Back in Benghazi we were all billeted in an Italian Army barracks which was absolutely crawling with fleas. Perhaps they were the Itis' secret weapons. Despite our lot looking a little ragged, we put on a big battalion parade for Prime Minister Robert Menzies. In his speech he made reference to the fact that he had flown over the desert following our line of advance. The usual voice from the back said: "Pity you hadn't walked over it". We were also visited by General Blamey (another battalion parade) who was full of praise for our efforts. We were pretty pleased with ourselves, too. Since that last day of December 1940 we had advanced almost 600 miles, a lot of it on our flat feet. Together with the 7th Armoured Division and the Northumberland Fusiliers, a machine gun battalion, we had defeated an army many times our size. Admittedly, the Italians were not a very determined enemy but, on a number of occasions, offered fierce resistance such as we encountered at Derna. We now had complete confidence in ourselves and our leaders.

The civilian population remained in Benghazi and the local government and police continued to administer the city under the direction of the garrison commander. We supplied security guards at all important facilities and street patrols to guard against looting. I was ordered – as corporal of a piquet (picket) of two men, plus an Italian policeman – to locate all the brothels and mark them on a map so that they could be inspected by the Medical Officer. It was a most interesting job and we were offered a number of "freebies" which, being on duty, we were obliged to decline.

We were now being subjected to air raids night and day, most of them concentrated on the harbour and surrounding areas. One day some of our platoon were on patrol when they encountered members of an Italian family crying and wailing in front of their home which had been partially destroyed by a bomb. They seemed to be indicating that there was somebody trapped inside the ruins so our blokes set to work tearing the wreckage apart. They eventually got to a room at the back when the women tore past them. They emerged triumphantly carrying a sewing machine.

The air raids became heavier and it was decided to move the battalion out of the city and back to the scrub, where we dug our slit trenches. At least they were free of fleas. Although not far out of the city, we camouflaged our position so well and did such a good job of hiding all our trucks under trees that we were overflown many times but never attacked.

Security guards and street patrols were still on duty in the city, but for those not involved it was a quiet restful period. Towards the end of February we farewelled Benghazi and returned to Gazala. We were there for about a week with nothing to do except rest. The only major concern was Italian "thermos bombs". These were innocuous looking things resembling thermos flasks, but if you picked up or kicked one it would explode. We sustained several casualties from these devices. Another innocent-looking but potentially lethal device was the "fountain pen" bomb which would explode when picked up, causing damage to hands and face.

After about a week we headed back to Tobruk to occupy some more flea-infested Italian dugouts. Then we moved again, this time to Mersa Matruh where we occupied clean British barracks, and were issued new clothing and our equipment brought up to scratch. We also got our kitbags back and I had my lion pyjamas again.

Then it was further back to El Amiriya, about 10 miles from Alexandria, and some well-earned leave. There was a canteen at Amiriya which served wonderful steak and eggs. We would have our dinner in camp and then head straight for another helping. The 9th Division blokes passed through on their way to the front and they looked on us with awe. We were the desert rats who had swept all before us in our victorious advance to Benghazi. They need not have felt that way because at Tobruk they withstood everything that Rommel could throw at them and beat him – the first and only defeat that he suffered before El Alamein, quite a long time later.

Chapter 5 - Derna, Benghazi And Back

CHAPTER 6
TO GREECE

In Alexandria we revelled in some marvellous leave. The city was full of bars and restaurants and with plenty of money in our pockets (for a change) we gave it a lively ride. I had my photograph taken and arranged for copies to be sent to Mum and Mary. As we had been warned to prepare for an imminent move I paid the photographer in advance and asked him to post them for me. I wasn't confident the pictures would ever arrive. However, I thought wrong of him and Mum and Mary got their photos in due course.

Our destination was Greece and it was a wonderful credit to our battalion that every man was present on parade before embarking, despite the fleshpots of Alexandria and the money to spend on them. We jammed into a Dutch ship called the *Pennland* together with the 2/8th Battalion, the 2/3rd Field Regiment and various headquarters personnel. The ship was overloaded by about a thousand men, and conditions were pretty uncomfortable. We spent most of the three-day voyage on deck where the wonderful sea air got rid of the desert dust out of our nostrils.

I can still remember my joy at spotting a Greek island for the first time from the deck. I never learned the island's name but recall a white road winding its way up a steep hill from the wharf; a road which only a donkey could have climbed. On the afternoon of the third day we sighted Athens and could see that awesome Greek monument, the Acropolis.

We received a wonderfully warm Greek welcome from the people who had gathered at the wharf and it was beaut to be amongst friendly civilians for the first time. From the port of Piraeus we went to the woods of Daphni where we were camped in tents under the trees close to a little stream. The official War History had this to say about it:

"What a contrast! Instead of awaking with eyes, ears and noses full of sand we breathed pure crisp air with the scent of flowers. Flowers! We hadn't seen them since leaving Australia. After months of desert glare the landscape at Daphni was a dream come true. The troops stood and gazed at the natural gardens full of shrubs and flowers which scented the breeze; at the grasses that made a swishing as you walked through … We saw civilians dressed as we used to dress before the war – civilians whom you could trust … From the hillside one could look back into the valley below and see Athens."

Those were the words of Lt Col C.H. Green (then a Captain in the 2/2nd Battalion), who was killed leading the 3rd Battalion R.A.R. in Korea in 1950.

The next day was spent on leave in Athens with strict orders to be back by midnight as we were to move out the next day. What a leave it was! We saw all the sights, including the Acropolis, and lunched and drank in the best hotels amidst wonderful hospitality. We socialised mostly with women and old men; the young men were fighting the Italians in Albania and making a pretty good job of it. Some of us visited a nightclub which put on a stage show that ended with two dancers on stage waving big British and Greek flags. The applause was prolonged and sincere. I got a real culture shock that evening. The club had one toilet to be shared by both sexes. It was, to say the least, rather off-putting to have women walking past as you stood at the urinal.

The next morning we went to the train station and piled into cattle trucks to start our trip north. The countryside was beautiful to behold. It was spring and the fruit trees were blooming, the fields were green; all with a backdrop of the snow-capped Pindus mountains. Every so often we would pass through a hamlet of little white, red-roofed houses where people, mainly women, lined the tracks trying to throw flowers into the trucks. What a pity, I thought, that we could not spend more time in this enchanting land of Greece.

We got out at Larissa, a fair sized town badly damaged by a recent earthquake. Companies were dispatched in various directions to guard important facilities against possible German paratroop attack. The next morning we were on the move again, heading north to the Yugoslav border as two German armoured divisions swept south towards the Monastir Gap in Yugoslavia, the pass through which ran the main road into Greece. If that force broke through and spread into the plains below before the Anzac Corps had time to establish a strong defensive line in the Mount Olympus area it would spell disaster because there were another four German divisions waiting to follow it in.

The Anzac force ordered to defend the Monastir position for three days consisted of the Rangers, a British battalion, the 2/8th and 2/4th Battalions. The Rangers drew the short straw by arriving first and were allotted the job of defending the floor of the pass. The 2/8th was on its right, up the slope, and we were on the left. We had a front of almost five miles to cover with only three rifle companies operating as C Company had been held by Force Headquarters. There was only enough signal cable to lay to A and B Companies. D Company, way out to the left, could only be reached by runner. It was snowing and bitterly cold. Gary Hart and I struggled through snow drifts to lay line to A Company, which was on the forward slope looking into Yugoslavia. From their position you could see the German divisions stretching for miles across the plains below. It was obvious, even to simple soldiers like us, that holding this horde for three days and four nights was not going to be easy.

The next day was Thursday April 10th. I remember it well because it was my 19th birthday. It was bitterly cold with a heavy, misty rain. That night was equally miserable. On Good Friday the weather worsened as a blizzard blew in and soaked us all. It was even worse for the rifle companies. Their slit trenches half filled with water as they peered through the mist to see if 'Jerry' was coming. He attacked late in the afternoon of the following day but was beaten off. The next day Jerry came again, launching very heavy attacks against B Company on the immediate left of the Rangers. The attacks were repulsed with heavy losses, but later in the day the German division smashed through the Rangers on the floor of the pass.

We were up against the SS Adolf Hitler Armoured Division which was one of the elite divisions of the German Army. With Jerry in the pass, both us and the 2/8th were left hanging out on a limb and in danger of being surrounded. Later that afternoon we received orders to withdraw. A and B Companies pulled back under very heavy fire, but the runner could not get through to D Company, way out to the left. We never heard from them again.

As we plodded down the road to our departure point we could hear a German tank clanking about trying to get around a crater in the road that had been blown by the engineers. When we got down to the plain – and on our way to safety – the battalion was stopped and turned back with orders to fight a rearguard action. In the original plan this was supposed to be the Rangers' job but they were no longer an effective force. By sheer chance we found a trench system, probably left over from a previous war, and we quickly occupied this good position above the river. A Greek food dump provided us with some loaves of bread but they were so hard you had to use a bayonet to penetrate the crust. Fortunately, the insides were all right, and being as hungry as bears, we wolfed it down. The signallers were now manning the trenches as riflemen. All our cable had been lost. The bridge over the river had been blown after we crossed it. A truck, presumably one of ours, came tearing down the road ahead of the Germans and went straight into the water. I didn't see what happened to whoever was inside. It was dark and we were trying to organise our defences.

The Germans now closed up to the far side of the river. We exchanged machine-gun and rifle fire but they made no attempt to cross to our side. It was dark and we weren't aware of the fact a group of our men was on the other side being held prisoner by the Germans. We discovered later that some of them had been wounded by our fire. After a sleepless night we were ordered to withdraw over the hill to where our transport was waiting. Heading up the hill, we came under heavy machine-gun fire but once again we were lucky. Jerry didn't have his range right and the bullets buzzed over our heads like bees. We piled into trucks and only then realised how completely exhausted we were.

The battalion suffered grievously at Monastir, losing more than a hundred men who were killed, wounded and missing (presumed captured), but we emerged from this trial by fire as a more cohesive, although reduced, battalion. In the withdrawal from Monastir, 9 Platoon of A Company had to hold a rearguard position to delay the Germans until the rest of the battalion got out. A member of this platoon, Dick Parry, later gave the following account of what happened on 12-13 April 1941:

"We have to take up a defensive position, while the rest of our troops get away, so once again we dig in at night on the side of a slope. We have lost our blankets and it's bitterly cold. We haven't closed our eyes for four nights, but the boys know what's coming in the morning, so they dig with a will with few picks and shovels.

"Mac and I have last use of the shovel in our section and we are only down about 18 inches when dawn breaks and there are the Huns just below us on the river. They open up and we crouch in our hole just below the surface. They have a body of men in front of them and seem to be driving towards us, sheltering behind them. We think they are our men being used as a human shield. Just then one of our Vickers guns opens up and the Huns and their shield go in all directions. Then follows an hour of the most concentrated fire I have ever experienced. They must have dozens of machine guns and can see us quite clearly on the fresh earth. The air becomes one whining, hissing mass of lead at a range of only a few hundred yards and we keep to the bottom of our shallow hole as bullets strike the parapet.

"At 7.30am word is passed from hole to hole to prepare to withdraw and we feel pretty shaky at the idea of having

to run some 300 yards up the slope through this inferno, completely exposed. The first man to poke his head up gets a bullet through it and drops back dead. Not so good. One after another the boys jump up and start to run and the volume of fire increases. I watch one of our section halfway back. As he runs the earth spurts all round him: he runs through it all and disappears over the rise, safe for the moment. It's my turn.

"I don't know what my thoughts were at this time – probably nil! I start to run but my legs simply refuse to function, so I have to walk. The bullets sing and whistle past. They thud on either side of me but I'm too exhausted to worry. A bloke in front of me falls and I catch up with him and try to help him. He is shot in the shoulder. He's bleeding badly and blood is spurting out of his boot. I give him a hand and we fall into a wadi, but he dies on the spot. They have a fixed line of fire up the wadi so I crawl out and over the hill where I find the rest of the platoon who were lucky enough to get out.

"Casualties: two killed, four wounded and worst of all one section did not get the order to withdraw and stayed there. They held up the Hun for another three hours and then most of them got out, though one of them was killed. Corporal Millard was very badly wounded in the arm and could not make the dash. Allan Manning would not leave him so both were taken prisoner. Just typical of Allan! We get into trucks which were waiting for us and are taken back to a mountain range near Servia Pass where the rest have already taken up positions. They give us gallons of tea and are really surprised to see us. They didn't expect us to survive our job of covering the withdrawal. Neither did we!"

Our Regimental Sergeant Major, Alfie Carpenter, came out of Monastir after the bridge was blown and had to swim the freezing river to get back to the battalion. The next morning he entered the river again to try and find a fording spot where he could get the transport out. Despite his best efforts he couldn't find one. That we got out at all was due, in large part, to the coolness and skill of our commanding officer. Colonel Dougherty always seemed to be in control of a most confused and difficult situation and his officers and men showed themselves capable of carrying out any task he gave them. Being in signals you were much more aware of what was going on in a tactical sense than anyone else in the battalion, with the exception of the intelligence section.

However, this small force of less than brigade strength had held the far superior enemy and bought the time necessary for the New Zealand and Australian battalions, well to our rear, to form a defensive line. We withdrew to the north of the Aliakmon River and moved to a spot up in the mountains to the left of the line. Fighting our weariness, we had to climb up to quite a height where we spent another cold night. At least it wasn't snowing!

Our orders were to cross the river, so the next morning we stumbled down the mountain to where the engineers had just finished building a trestle bridge. Despite little equipment, they did a marvellous job for the river was very wide. We crossed the swaying structure to the safety of the far bank and began a steep climb which took us most of the day. Transport was waiting at the top and I climbed into a small truck with the CO and a few other officers. After a hairy ride down the other side of the mountain, we stopped at Domokos where we transferred to another fleet of trucks. Some of our platoon boarded a New Zealand truck which, for some strange reason, took them all the way to Athens. I wouldn't see John Meehan, Bruce Cork, Selby Dean and a few other mates until after the war.

We were sent all the way back to Brallos Pass to another defensive position, stopping briefly at Larissa near an abandoned NAAFI canteen. There were cigarettes, liquor and plenty of other goodies for the taking. You could only take what you could carry so I settled for a bottle of whisky and a tin of sausages.

On top of being hit by an earthquake, Larissa had been heavily bombed and was in a hell of a mess. One member of our platoon, who shall remain nameless, came across a jeweller's shop which had taken a direct hit from a bomb. Jewellery was scattered everywhere and he picked up a very expensive-looking diamond necklace and stuffed it in his haversack, thinking it would bring a good price back in Cairo. He was being evacuated from Greece on an old tub called the *Costa Rica* when a German Stuka (a dive bomber) came out of the sun and dropped his bomb. It narrowly missed the ship but exploded so close that it sprung the plates and the vessel started to sink. Everybody was ordered on deck and destroyers came along side to take them off. Our man was in a quandary. In the bowels of the ship was his haversack with the precious diamond necklace but the ship had sunk to such an extent that men were simply jumping onto the decks of the destroyers. He made his decision and the necklace is now on the bottom of the Mediterranean somewhere south of Crete.

The cloudy and rainy days meant the German Air Force had not been a problem, but once the weather improved their Stukas bombed and strafed truck convoys on the roads from first to last light. Stukas were fitted with a screaming device which was turned on when they dived and this did have an effect on troop morale. Surprisingly, these attacks did not cause a lot of casualties for as soon as the planes appeared everybody jumped out of the trucks and took cover on the sides of the roads. However, when a road was cratered or trucks hit and destroyed, quick movement was difficult. Our fighter cover was now non-existent, having either been shot down or destroyed on the ground.

Thermopylae is a narrow strip of land between the sea and Brallos Pass where Leonidas and his Spartans had fought to the last man against Persian invaders well before the birth of Christ. The road from Lamia to Brallos is long and straight and the Stukas gave us hell. They were able to fly directly down the road so if they missed the truck they were aiming at, the bomb would probably hit the one in front or behind. Eventually we crossed the Sperchios River and headed up the mountain to Brallos. Here the battalion dug into positions overlooking that long, straight road to Lamia. Our platoon commander, Lt Claude Raymond, had by some miracle got his hands on some cable and we were able to connect up A and B Companies. B Company was on the road near two 25-pounder guns which were sited in an exposed position so that they could fire on the bridge over the Sperchios. This time the New Zealanders had drawn the short straw and were down on the flat at Thermopylae. It was obvious that the main German attack would be directed at them.

In the mountains to our left the Greek Army was disintegrating. We received news that the Greek government was going to capitulate and wanted the allied forces to evacuate the country. It was, therefore, essential that the position at Thermopylae be held as long as it took to get all the other troops to ports and beaches where they could be taken off by ships.

The two 25-pounders were effectively preventing Jerry from crossing the bridge over the Sperchios so he brought up a battery of 15cm (6″) guns to try and silence them. Shortly after he commenced firing the line to B Company went dead. I set out to find the break and repair it, having a fair idea where it would be. Sure enough, just across the road the cable had been cut by shellfire. The entire area was lousy with shell-holes, but I had a clear view of the break.

I scrambled over to the cable and had just finished mending the break when I heard the guns fire again so I went face down on the ground. In what is undoubtedly the luckiest moment of my life, a bracket of four shells came screaming in and landed all around me. The closest one wouldn't have been any more than 10 to 15 yards away, perhaps even closer. The ear-splitting explosions knocked me out. When I came around I found myself flat on my back. The blast had scorched the left side of my face, giving me a bit of a haircut. I knew immediately that I had been hit in the chest. There wasn't much blood, and it wasn't painful – that came later. At the time I was relieved I had escaped with so little damage. I didn't realise until long after the war that the hearing in my left ear was no good.

I scrambled down to B Company Headquarters where Jack Huston put a field dressing on me; then calmly helped me back to battalion headquarters. On the way I passed Pop Lilyman. "Pop there's a bottle of my whisky in my pack," I said. "Take it and drink it." If anyone loved Scotch whisky, it was Pop! I didn't drink a lot then. Perhaps it was me who really felt like he needed one?

At the RAP they poured half a bottle of iodine into the wound, bandaged me up, put me into an ambulance and sent me down to the casualty clearing station on the plain below. I was left on a stretcher in the open and German planes, on sighting the big Red Cross on the ground, left us alone. When it got dark the flashes of the guns lit up the sky from where I had been and it was wonderful to feel so safe and to dream of clean sheets, and lovely nurses in a safe and secure hospital.

Unfortunately, this was not the case for in the back areas troops were being evacuated and a certain amount of chaos reigned. During the night three of us were put into an ambulance for the trip to the 26th General Hospital in Athens which was a British facility still in operation. The other two men were pretty badly wounded and were far worse off than me. They must have had a fair bit of morphine in them because they got through the trip without too much trouble.

Early in the morning we pulled into Athens' Omonia Square. The medical orderly opened the doors of the ambulance so that we could get a breath of fresh air. Greek women rushed up and threw flowers in until the floor of the ambulance was covered and a beautiful scent filled the air. The hospital was overflowing and I ended up on a stretcher in a corridor. A couple of doctors examined me and asked me if I could walk. When I said yes they marked me for evacuation and that night I went by truck to Megara, a beach south of Athens. Here I was, overjoyed to meet up with my battalion which was also to be taken off from this beach. All the next day we took cover under the trees in an olive grove. There was plenty of enemy air activity but we managed to avoid their interest.

It was now that I made one of the worst mistakes of my life. I should have stayed with the battalion, which was poised to board the waiting destroyers, using rope ladders. The wounded were to go on another ship which had easier loading facilities. I thought that I could probably handle a rope ladder; and in any case I had plenty of mates who would have helped me. But the dream of clean sheets and lovely nurses must have still have had a strong hold on me because I decided to stay with the wounded. That night we were assembled into groups of about 40 ready to depart. Rusty McWilliam was also in my group and at 3.00am we had reached the water's edge. Then, with sinking heart, I read the Aldis lamp from the ship which simply said "ship full". Rusty and I had a short conference. "I'll be buggered if I'm going to hang around and get taken prisoner," I said.

We headed back to the road to see if we could find a vehicle going south. An ambulance came along and Rusty stood in the middle of the road to make him stop. "I can't take you I'm full," said the driver. But Rusty was nothing if not persuasive. I got in the front and sat on the passenger's lap. Rusty stood on the running board.

At Corinth, about 50 miles southwest of Athens, there was a canal, wide enough to take a reasonable ship, spanned by a bridge. We had just got to the far side when we heard planes. Above us at a height of about 500 feet roared a mass of German Junkers discharging paratroopers. The paratroopers were dropped on both sides of the steel bridge and began landing just a couple of hundred yards away from us. Shots were going everywhere. Just then the bridge was blown by the engineers, cutting off one lot of paratroopers, but that still left enough of them on our side to worry us. Everybody scrambled out of the ambulance and scattered in all directions and that is when I lost Rus.

We came under fire and as we had no weapons we beat it south down the road away from the bridge. We could hear some vehicles coming up behind us and could only presume they were German so dived for cover off the side of the road till they passed. They were Germans on motor bikes with side cars and a machine gun mounted on the side car which must have been dropped with them.

Meanwhile, I discovered later, Rusty was on the move. A quick-thinking man with great initiative, he eventually made his way to the last evacuation point at Kalamata. When he got there he found thousands of men between him and the water. A naval officer appeared accompanied by a petty officer and an army sergeant, no doubt assessing how many troops they could evacuate that night. The naval officer was the Beachmaster. When they turned to go back to the beach, Rusty simply hooked on the rear of the party. The mass of men parted like the Red Sea and in no time he was at the embarkation point. "Where do the walking wounded go, mate?" he asked a naval officer. "In that boat over there, cobber," came the reply. So he hopped in and ended up in Alexandria. After the war I told him I knew why he got out of Greece and I didn't – he was one hell of a lot smarter!

For me there was clearly no future in staying near the road so another bloke and I headed for the hills, knowing that Jerry would have enough on his plate. From what I can remember, the man with me was a bombardier with the British Armoured Brigade. We were halfway up the hill when he announced that he had enough of this nonsense and was going down to give himself up. The irony of it all was that he had a large tattoo on his arm which read: "Death before Dishonour".

Chapter 6 - To Greece

CHAPTER 7

ON THE RUN

I climbed very slowly to the top of the hill and looked down on the town (which I found out later was Nafplion) and harbour below. A ship, the *Ulster Prince*, was burning there. It seemed very unlikely that evacuation from that port would be possible.

I took stock of my situation and it was all a bit depressing. My wound wasn't troubling me too much, but the shell splinter was still lodged in my chest. The injury had not been dressed since the day it happened. Now it was discharging and it smelled. I only had the clothes I stood up in and my shirt was bloodstained with a hole in it. Fortunately my boots and socks were in good condition.

There was only one thing to do and that was to keep heading south so I started following a track through the hills. After a period of slow progress, I came to a little village of about four houses. A Greek family took me in, showered me with kindness and dished up a meal of eggs, bread, olives and milk. I had not eaten for nearly two days and this simple food tasted like caviar. Afterwards I bedded down on the floor and fell fast asleep. While I slept one of the women took away my shirt and when I awoke in the morning it had been washed and the hole mended.

After a breakfast of bread, cheese and milk an old man put me on a donkey and began walking me down the track. About two hours later we stopped and he indicated, by sign language, that he was going back. Left on my own, I pushed on to the next village where I was again the recipient of some wonderful, warm Greek kindness. In this way I moved from village to village till I reached a fairly big one. Here a most attractive young woman was brought to me. She was the local school teacher and could speak very good English. The next day she took me down the mountain to a spot where we could look down on the Aegean Sea and the island of Spetses. We sat on a rock beside a little stream and talked for quite a while about this calamity that had come to the Greek people and ourselves, and what we might do after this war was over. I deeply regret that I could not take her name and address. I didn't want to run the risk of being captured and the Germans discovering her identity.

In hindsight the least I could have done was memorise the name of her village, but I was thinking only of myself and how I was going to get away. I left her there and walked down to the water to catch the ferry to Spetses. As I waited a group of giggling prostitutes turned up, probably from a brothel somewhere nearby. They, too, were trying to get away from the advancing Germans.

On Spetses, I asked, by sign language, if there was a hospital in the vicinity. A Greek woman took me to a small white building on the waterfront where I was examined by a young doctor who spoke very good English.

He deadened the whole wound area with an anaesthetic spray and went in with a long pair of forceps. I could hear clinking as he poked around and eventually he pulled a fair-sized shell splinter out and gave it to me. I still have that metal fragment with me today; a vivid reminder of how lucky I was to avoid death at the hands of a German artillery battery.

Another half-bottle of iodine and a new dressing later and I was on my way. I chose a house at random where I asked a Greek woman if she could provide me with a bed for the night. Like every Greek I had struck, she was all kindness. Soon I was tucked up in a bed made up with some lovely clean sheets. At last I had found them. In the morning the woman (I never found out her name) told me that her husband had been a major in the Greek army before he was killed in the battle of Koritsa in Albania.

If there was anything that could have topped the clean sheets it was that wonderful morning bath. I hadn't washed for so long I could barely remember how. Before I left, the woman gave me some shaving gear that had belonged to her late husband, a towel, some soap, a loaf of bread, cheese and a small sack in which to carry it all. She also told me that there were quite a few soldiers in Spetses. After thanking her for her great kindness to me, I went to find them.

It wasn't long before I linked up with about 40 Allied soldiers, mostly British and Australian, and a British officer, Lt. Col. Courage, who had enough cash to hire a boat to ferry us to the island of Milos. Why we didn't head straight for Crete I would never know. But when you are separated from your battalion you lose confidence in the decisions made by other officers. Still, I suppose they have their problems.

That evening we set sail, jammed like sardines into a caique (cargo boat). Just before dawn we reached a small island. We scrambled off the boat and took cover under some trees with orders not to look up if an aircraft came over because faces could be easily spotted from the air. Planes flew over twice that day but evidently did not notice us. After dusk we set off again and into a severe storm. The boat tossed about like a cork. We were all quickly soaked by the spray flying over the boat but by first light the storm had gone and the sea had calmed. A few hours later we were standing on Milos. The boat returned to Spetses that evening, leaving a couple of us perturbed enough to approach the Colonel and ask him why the captain wasn't made to take us to Crete. His response was all very stiff upper lip. The Colonel said he had only contracted the ship to take us to Milos and it would not be right to make the captain go any further. This decidedly British attitude was "play up, play up and play the game". I believe our CO, in the same position, would have only been thinking of his men and how he could best get them to safety. Unfortunately he wasn't there.

For the next week we based ourselves on a beach on the other side of the harbour from the town as efforts were made to repair the diesel engine of a large boat which had been bought using funds held by the Colonel. Food was running short but we managed to replenish our rations with food we bought from the local Greeks. In an effort to improve our diet, I headed inland with another bloke, who had a rifle, to find and shoot a sheep. The only thing we could cook it in was a steel helmet, but the varnish went right through the meat and made it taste awful. Again, we were only thinking of ourselves and not the poor farmer who owned the sheep. At last it was announced that the engine had been fixed and we all clambered aboard our boat and went down into the hold. The engine kicked over. It seemed that we were at last on our way to freedom when on the ladder leading down into the hold there suddenly appeared a highly-polished pair of short jack boots.

The boots adorned the feet of a well-dressed German naval officer. He was unarmed and, I later learned, hailed from a destroyer that had crept unannounced into the port. He pointed to one of our lot, a red-haired Englishman, and said, in quite clear English: "Stand up you". He did as he was ordered and the German officer asked him if he was "Englander". He replied: "No, me Greek", and that was the end of the caper. We were immediately ordered off. If any of us had any thoughts of trying to tackle him, we kept them to ourselves. We knew there would be plenty more Germans waiting for us. On deck we couldn't miss the destroyer, or the armed naval ratings waiting to escort us off.

As we trudged up the hill to the local school a confused bundle of recriminatory thoughts rushed through my mind. Why couldn't the engine of the boat have been fixed the day before? How the hell did I ever get mixed up with this motley mob? Why didn't Col. Courage have the courage to make the captain of the boat that brought us to Milos take us on to Crete? It didn't matter what I thought. The fact remains that I was caught fair and square and, as far as I know, became one of the very few Australian soldiers to be captured by the German Navy!

CHAPTER 8

PRISONER OF WAR

As I sat with my fellow prisoners, crowded into that small Greek classroom, an unbelievable feeling of depression and shame came over me. It was the 9th of May, 1941, a date I would never forget.

When I'd had the time to think about what might happen to me during the war, becoming a prisoner of war had never really entered my mind. When reality hit it was devastating to me that I might never see my mates again. It was raining that morning and I couldn't help but recall the words of English poet Siegfried Sassoon writing about World War I in his poem *Sick Leave*:

"In bitter safety I awake unfriended
And as the dawn begins with slashing rain
I think of the battalion in the mud."

The island of Milos, famed as the home of the legendary Venus de Milo, was the cursed island as far as we were concerned; one from which we could not escape and which had become our prison. The sense of guilt and shame was still strong; that I had failed as a soldier, failed my mates and failed myself.

The Germans brought more men to the island to build an airstrip and set the POWs and most of the adult Greeks to work as labourers. The level area chosen for the strip was covered with rocks which all had to be carried to the side of the area where the planes would land. To be honest, Jerry was very good to me and regularly dressed my wound which by now had almost healed. I didn't have to work, but was taken out every day with the rest of the POWs.

Because it was quite flat, with an approach from the sea, it didn't take long to make the ground good enough for light aircraft to land. Apparently several months earlier the RAF had visited the island and decided that it was an unsuitable site for a landing field. Shortly after the airstrip was finished we were loaded onto an old Greek freighter and sailed to Piraeus where another load of POWs were herded on board. We were imprisoned down in the hold, which was very crowded and hot, and only allowed out to go to the toilet – a wooden structure hanging over the side. We reached Salonika a very thirsty and hungry lot.

The camp at Salonika was an old Greek cavalry barracks infested with fleas and lice. This was our first encounter with lice and we soon found that they could persistently torment the hell out of you. There was very little food except for one day when we received a good serving of horse meat stew, which was absolutely delicious. Some of the blokes were a bit hesitant about eating one of man's best friends but when you are close to starving you will consume anything edible. A lot of men had stomach complaints and dysentery started to become a problem. A large group of us were taken down to the wharves to help load ships and, lo and behold, my party was the one ordered to load 15cm shells which I understood to be for the same battery that shot me up at Brallos Pass.

Although my wound was virtually healed, the Germans were very fair to me. I didn't have to heave the heavy shells around but was given light duties instead.

In camp our living condition were getting gradually worse as our food supply dwindled. Our usual ration was a bowl of lentil soup each day and a loaf of bread between four men. Sometimes we got a bit of horse meat. Generous Greek women started throwing bread over the wire, defying the guards who would hit them with rifle butts if they could catch them. Even so, they would keep coming back. There was, of course, a mad scramble for the bread and you would have to be very lucky to get some.

One night an English officer, a Lt Hornby of the Hornby model train family, tried to escape by climbing over the barbed wire. A German guard, armed with a Schmeisser sub-machine gun, riddled him with bullets. That was the only escape attempt that I was aware of at that camp. We heard the shots that night didn't know what had happened. As far as I was concerned, it was simply foolhardy trying to get over the wire. If I was going to escape I would have to be smarter.

After a couple of weeks in that stinking place we were moved to Salonika No. 2 which was even worse. This had also been a Greek cavalry barracks and the Germans had procured some very nice looking horses which they kept in the stables. A party of us was detailed to muck out. The officer overseeing the stables was a blond haired, blue eyed bastard who picked fault with everything. It was the first time I'd had a close acquaintance with a German soldier and I found him very arrogant. His was a beautiful white horse and everything about its grooming, gear and stable had to be perfect. When we weren't working in the stables we would sit in the sun, strip off our clothes, get the lice out of the seams and crush them. This, with a bit of luck, might mean a couple of hours sleep before they were back again.

An audacious but disastrous escape attempt was made when someone came across a manhole to a sewer which was believed to connect to another manhole outside the camp. A large group of men gathered round the manhole to hide their activity from the guards and a number went down. Somehow Jerry found out and sent some men to the exit point were they started shooting up the pipe. This caused some casualties while also panicking the men at that end into trying desperately to get back. Meanwhile, men from the camp end pressed on and there was a terrible traffic jam in the middle. Some were suffocated by the fumes and the whole enterprise failed miserably. I didn't like that proposition from the start. I was claustrophobic and the fumes were bad.

Most of us now had either diarrhea or dysentery, with some POWs even perishing from the latter it was so bad. After about three weeks in that cursed place we were informed that we were going to Germany and marched down to the railway station. We were given a half-loaf of bread, three army biscuits, a bottle of water and a small tin of meat and loaded in – about 50 to a cattle truck. We didn't know then that the food and water had to last us for five days. There was no room to lie down. Those around the sides were the luckiest as they could rest their backs. The only sanitary facilities were a bucket and a jam tin in the corner near the small window. It was now mid-summer and it very quickly got very hot. The stench from the toilet bucket – used by so many men with diarrhea – was almost overpowering. Looking back this was probably when I was at my lowest ebb. I had never felt such a long way from Australia. Yet, although freedom seemed such a long way off, even then I was never pessimistic about the final outcome. Even while squeezed into that cattle truck, with that horrendous smell in my nostrils, I just knew it would turn out all right in the end.

After about three days my food ran out but fortunately I still had some water. At Belgrade the Yugoslav Red Cross was waiting with some soup but, as luck would have it, the supply ran out before they reached our truck. The crowded conditions meant good sleep was impossible and we were a very tired, hungry and thirsty mob. After five seemingly endless days and nights, we reached Stalag 18A at Wolfsberg in Austria. Thank goodness we weren't travelling further into Germany. As we crawled out of that stinking hellhole of a truck we saw the most wonderful thing in the world – a tap with running water. We went to the delousing area where we were showered and our clothes were fumigated. The Germans were terrified of typhus which was carried by lice.

My good mate Joe Wishart's trip was even more eventful. Shortly after leaving Salonika, Joe somehow managed to squeeze through the small window of the cattle truck. He clung on to the side of the truck until he spotted a clear space and then let go. As he rolled over and over, the guard, who was in a raised structure at the back of the truck saw him. He fired several shots but missed and Joe ran off to temporary freedom. Despite hurting his arm, Joe was on the run for several days before he was picked up by a German patrol, returned to Salonika and put on another train. For this and a number of other escape attempts, he was awarded the British Empire Medal – one of the very few to receive a decoration for service while a prisoner of war.

The German invasion of Russia had resulted in the capture of hundreds of thousands of prisoners, with some sent to a compound at Wolfsberg. The French had occupied their own large compound since 1940. A smaller compound housed a number of Yugoslavs. The Australian, British and Kiwi POWs were the last to arrive, meaning we were placed in new huts which, after fumigation, meant there were no fleas, bed bugs or lice. Each hut held about a hundred men. The wooden bunks were large enough to sleep three on each level. The man in the middle drew the short straw as he had to climb out the end. Basic washing facilities and a large urinal bucket for night-time were also provided. The latrine was a long trench with a pole to sit on. The local farmers regularly scooped the sewage out the trench and took it away to put on their crops. We thought this was pretty disgusting but apparently it was common practice in European peasant farming.

The food was much better than we had been living on since being captured. Each morning we were given a loaf of bread large enough for six men. Cutting this into equal portions required great skill as the bread was shaped like a Vienna loaf. Syndicates of six men were formed and the most precise became the cutter. Sometimes we were also given a small piece of cheese or sausage and a cup of foul-tasting ersatz coffee. At midday we marched in threes down to the cookhouse for our main meal of the day which was usually stew and often quite tasty. The problem was if you had eaten all your bread that was all you had until the next day. Blokes with great self-discipline were able to keep some back for an evening meal but I found this very hard to do.

Russia had not signed the Geneva Conventions and its POWs, who had been very harshly treated before they got to the camp, received far fewer rations than we did. They died in large numbers. So desperate were the Russian POWs for food that they marched to the cookhouse in threes with a dead prisoner in the middle, allowing his mates to collect his rations as well. The Germans quickly woke up to this ploy and stopped it.

Every morning a German civilian would arrive with a horse and cart at the gate of the Russian compound. Prisoners who had survived the night would load onto the cart those who had died since the previous day. Where and how they were buried we didn't know, but it's a sure bet there was no ceremony attached to it. The families of these poor unfortunates would most likely never know what happened to them and that is terribly sad. I had no knowledge of the Holocaust during my time as a POW but I can say that our German captors' indifference to the suffering of the Russian POWs was horribly cruel and inhumane. We did, however, get a strong indication of the German obsession with hunting down Jews. All the Allied prisoners at the camp were forced to have their penis inspected. Those who were circumcised were subjected to an interrogation about their family history. How the Germans would know they were being told the truth was something I never quite understood.

The summer and autumn of 1941 was the very low point of the war and we could all see we were in for a long period behind barbed wire. There was no pessimism about this and practically without exception we were confident that we would win this war. We tried to convey this confidence to the German guards whenever we could, but they would have none of it. Why would they? At this time they were winning everywhere and strongly believed that their Führer would lead them to final victory. 'Sieg Heil' and all that! At this stage we had no clandestine radio and the only news we got was from a camp newspaper which was published by the Germans. This contained glowing reports of victories on all fronts which were probably fairly true but on principle we wouldn't believe them.

Stalag 18A was a main camp from which men were sent out to smaller work camps or Arbeitskommandos. I was one of a group of about one hundred loaded into cattle trucks and sent off to Spittal. From there we marched about two miles to Groppenstein, where we were put to work building a road that was to run from Spittal to Salzburg. We were housed in barracks, about 20 to a room, with upper and lower bunks and straw mattresses. Until then our only clothing had been what we were wearing when taken prisoner. All of us looked rather ragged and our boots were close to worn out. Fortunately, it was still the end of summer and the weather was mild. At the barracks we were issued with French uniforms of various styles and colours which had the effect of making us look like a troupe of musical comedy characters. Instead of boots we were issued with clogs and fusslappen which were pieces of flannel that you were wrapped around your feet instead of socks. To the uninitiated, clogs are very hard to wear. There was no give in them, making it very easy to slip or to sprain your ankle. No wonder we preferred our worn boots. The barracks boasted a well-equipped kitchen and the food was fair. Sadly, a young New Zealander working in the kitchen decided to help himself to too much horse meat out of the stew. He died in agony from a twisted bowel. We had very little meat and I believe he must have overdone it.

I was put to work cracking rocks with a sledgehammer. The only experience I had of this sort of thing was watching movies that featured convicts in chain gangs. It was certainly not as easy as it looked on screen. Eventually I was shown how to find the grain in the rock and how to split it. Just as I had a handle on that our group was sent to another section of the road where we were put to work digging and cutting through a small hill. The only machinery that used petrol was a small engine used to pull the skips loaded with spoil and the steam roller. The shot holes for blasting were all drilled by hand. One man hit the long drill with a hammer and the other turned the bit after each hit. A long scoop helped remove the stone dust. The worst job was holding the drill. You just hoped the striker wouldn't miss.

One thing I'll never forget from this experience was the sight one of an immaculate German officer wandering past us one day with a lovely looking young woman on his arm. He stopped, turned to one side and had a leak, with his companion – eyes averted – still standing there. Such a complete lack of modesty amazed us.

One member of our gang was a New Zealander, Bill Keith, who was a 'navvy', (a labourer) in civilian life. He taught me how to use a long-handled shovel which made life a lot easier. Bill regaled us with stories, including one about the time he was working on a farm. Quite often when he and the farmer, whose name was John, were out working, the farmer's wife would come down to the edge of the field and call out: "John, I'm going in to town. Do you want the use of my body before I go?" Small moments of amusement like this helped us get through the day.

We were determined to work as slowly as possible so as to make the smallest contribution to the German war effort. However, you had to be careful not to provoke too much of a reaction from the German guard or the foreman. It was also remarkably difficult to work slowly all the time. It seemed an unnatural thing to do.

We worked on a section of road about 300-400m long. After preparing the bed, we laid rocks with the ends pointing upwards before going along with a hammer and knocking all the tops off to create a level surface. It was hard work because you couldn't kneel to do it. Once that was done the whole area was covered with blue metal and crushed with a roller. Then some sort of road base material was put on top and rolled in. In my time, no bitumen or concrete was laid, but probably this came later. Almost entirely built by hand, it was a good piece of road and I have no doubt that it would last for many years, although we took no pride in its construction.

October was upon us and winter was approaching. It had started to get quite cold when, wonder of wonders, we each received a Red Cross food parcel and a marvellous supply of clothing – a British battledress, shirts and socks. God bless the International Red Cross! The best thing of all was a pair of British army boots. All this could not have come at a better time. We didn't know it then but the winter we were facing was to be the most severe for many years; something the German Army experienced at great cost when a great part of it almost perished in the bitter cold outside Moscow. Hitler believed that the war would be over before winter set in and his troops had no winter clothing. Apparently German women were asked to donate their fur coats to rectify the situation. One could just imagine a German Digger sitting in his frozen slit trench with a mink coat on!

As we progressed deeper into winter our working conditions worsened. Overnight the work face would freeze to a depth of about a metre. It then had to be drilled – by hand, of course – and then blown to make the face workable. We were supplied with gloves because if the temperature plunged below zero and we grabbed hold of metal with bare hands our skin would stick to it. Meals were brought to us at about midday and were usually cold before arriving. Usually it was soup or a thin stew. One day I looked down at my food and there was a sheep's eye staring back at me. As hungry as I was, I couldn't stomach it. "Does anybody want this," I asked. One of my workmates had no such reservations. "Give it to me," he said, before snatching it up and wolfing it down.

The Germans now decided that if the temperature was less than –28 degrees Celsius we did not have to start work till 10.00am. This was probably more of a concession to the guards and the civilians than the POWs. Each room at the barracks had a 44-gallon drum filled with sawdust and a length of galvanised pipe down the middle. The sawdust was lit at the bottom and burned slowly. When it really got going you could stir it up by jiggling the pipe. The warmth it gave off was a real godsend as the weather got colder and colder.

Our room consisted of a pretty good bunch of blokes, an almost even number of British, New Zealanders and Aussies. One Englishman, Dale Cornish, entertained us with stories of his life as a chauffeur. He was employed when his boss got his first car. They were driving in the country when the motor started to play up. His boss rapped on the glass partition and asked what the trouble was. Dale told him that he thought a sparkplug was missing. He was rebuked and told that it was his responsibility to make sure that no one stole anything from the car.

Conversations helped pass the time. As we earnestly discussed what had happened in Greece and Crete we realised we had been sacrificial lambs to the slaughter. The Australians and New Zealanders were particularly bitter as they felt they had done most of the fighting without any protection from the air against a superbly equipped enemy of overwhelming strength, including tanks. In the process, two fine infantry divisions were practically destroyed for no good result. We knew that our Commander-in-Chief, Tom Blamey, was strongly against the venture but British Prime Minister Winston Churchill persisted. He was certainly not the flavour of the month with Australian troops.

Toothache had become a big problem and after numerous requests the camp commandant finally announced that a doctor was coming up from Spittal to attend to our teeth. Those in need lined up outside an office with a large window. The first man in indicated which tooth was aching. The doc took a pair of forceps out of his bag, locked onto the molar and yanked it straight out. "Next," said the guard. Strangely, all the onlookers had disappeared. In time a few did return. The POW who went first later said that, after the first shock and pain, he had suffered no bad after-effects.

By now more Red Cross food parcels were getting through and for the first time were getting almost enough food. The Canadian food parcels were more prized than those from England. Still, I suppose the Canadians were not suffering food shortages. More cigarettes were particularly welcome as winter dragged on.

As spring approached a young POW's fancy turned not to love but the possibility of escape. The bloke in the bunk above me was Bill Grattan-Wilson a Victorian from, I believe, the 2/6th Battalion. After many long discussions we decided we would give it a burl as soon as the weather got a bit warmer. In hindsight we rather stupidly planned a route across the north of Italy into southern France which was then still relatively unoccupied by the Germans – a very ambitious venture indeed. We would have been far better off heading to Switzerland. Bill and I started saving tinned food from our Red Cross parcels and any other non-perishable items we could get our hands on.

Around the beginning of April 1942 we decided we make a run for it at the earliest possible opportunity. It was a nerve-wracking decision because no-one had escaped from the camp before and we did not know of anyone anywhere who had pulled off a successful escape. Questions loomed in my mind. What would happen to us if we were caught? Would we be shot? Eventually we pushed our fears aside, if only temporarily, and decided to go on a Sunday. This was a no-work day and there would be plenty of movement in the camp to hide our activity.

CHAPTER 9
ON THE RUN AGAIN

Off the kitchen there was a fairly large room which we were allowed to use for a couple of hours at night to play cards or have a sing-song. Bill and I got our gear down to the room by walking there surrounded by a number of men. There was one guard who patrolled the entire perimeter of the camp and it took him quite a while to do this. There were about 100 POWs in this camp and all of them started to sing to hide the noise. We threw our packs out the window and then tumbled out after them. The guard was at the back of the camp and out of sight, so we cut the wire with a pair of stolen pliers and crawled through. We repaired the wire as best we could so it would not be too obvious and scuttled down the hill. It was wonderful to feel some sort of freedom. As we hurried down the hill towards the River Drau we could hear the others singing the number made famous by Gracie Fields: *Wish Me Luck As You Wave Me Goodbye.*

"Wish me luck, as you wave me goodbye.
Cheerio, here I go, on my way.

Wish me luck as you wave me goodbye.
With a cheer, not a tear, make it gay.

Give me a smile, I can keep for a while,
In my heart while I'm away.

Till we meet once again you and I,
Wish me luck as you wave me goodbye."

It was about 7.50pm and the POWs would all have to be back in the barracks at 8.00pm. Lights-out was at 9.00pm and the guards would check each room before that to make sure that everybody was in bed. Our beds were made up with dummies. Whether this worked I don't know because I never saw anybody from the camp again.

We crossed the Drau about midnight – I slipped and fell in but fortunately it wasn't too cold. Bill and I kept heading west as quickly as we could to get as far away from Groppenstein as possible. Just before first light we climbed up the mountainside and camped for the day amongst some big rocks. In Austria, and presumably in Europe generally, most people live in valleys surrounded by steep and thickly wooded mountains. As we were in uniform our plan was to travel during the night and sleep in the hills during the day. There were two ways of travelling. One was to dress in civilian clothes, but the disadvantage was you could be mistaken for being a spy and have to prove you were an escapee. Travelling in uniform limited your movements, to only during night, but at least if you were picked up it was obvious who you were.

It was now April 10th – my 20th birthday – and we had been on the run for three days. At least I could celebrate my birthday in comparative freedom after being a POW for almost exactly a year.

We were heading for the Plocken Pass which led into Italy. At one stage we had to walk through a small village in the middle of the night and there were men going to work at a nearby sawmill but they took no notice of us. At one time it was very dark and I climbed up a signpost to read what it said and it fell over. We tried to put it back into position. We were moving at a good rate, although our progress was not exactly fast because movement in the dark was difficult and we had to give ourselves plenty of time in the darkness to get well up into the hills to find a suitable hiding place. Similarly, it took a fair while to get down in the valley for the next night's walk. Bill was quite a bit older then me and, although a bit religious, was a real good bloke and we got on very well which was very important on this sort of venture. On later escape attempts there were times when I wished that I had Bill with me again.

We had been on the run for seven days and were in sight of Oberdrauburg. South of that town was the Pass. Our map told us there was a road running along the border which would get us there. On the eighth night we climbed up to the top of the range and found the road. We had to go through the village of Koetschach which we knew was near our destination. It was very cold and there was a fair bit of ice on the road because of the altitude. We spent a cold day amongst some rocks just off the road and failed to get much sleep. After eight days we were close to the border. That night, shortly after setting out, we came to a road running south which our map told us led to Plocken Pass. It was a steep climb and a tricky one with the ice that was about. Suddenly, we were looking into Italy and got a very unpleasant surprise. The German hillsides were covered in thick forest – ideal for a prisoner of war to hide in. On the Italian side, their hills were as bare as a badger's bum.

We ventured off the road for a while until we came upon an Austrian cemetery from World War I. We sat amongst the tombstones and considered our options. We didn't have many. There was an Italian border post but no German one. We decided to try and sneak around the post and set out, sliding on the ice as we went. On the left side we came to a steep drop so retreated and tried the other side.

We were almost past the post when we were sprung and what seemed like half the Italian Army came pouring out of their positions and surrounded us. An Italian officer, who looked like a General but was in fact a Lieutenant, spoke some English and we were able to convey that we were prisoners of war. We were kept under close guard all night and the next morning taken by truck to what appeared to be their headquarters in the valley. There we were interrogated by this magnificent looking creature who spoke good English.

We found, as with the Germans, that it was useless trying to tell them that we were Australian. We were either Englander or Inglesi. Most of them didn't even know where Australia was. They didn't know what you were talking about and after a while you just had to tell them you were Englander. That went a bit against the grain. Sometimes you tried to explain but they really didn't know much about what was outside Europe.

We were taken by truck on a fairly long trip to an Udine civilian jail which looked just like Long Bay or Sing Sing. We were put in a cell with an English Sergeant who had also escaped from Germany. We were again interrogated and told that we would be sent back to Germany. It would be another month before we were actually sent packing. After more than a week on short rations we were pretty hungry but Udine was certainly

Charles on the farm in Blaxland,
New South Wales around 1927,
with a reluctant Bluey.

Charles's battalion, the 2/4th Battalion, marching past
Sydney Town Hall, January 1940.

Charles heading off to war on board
the *Strathnaver*, departing from
Pyrmont, 10 January, 1940.

The *Strathnaver* at sea, with 6 Platoon on
"A" Deck; training in full swing.

On 30 March, 1941 the author was on leave in Alexandria under 12 hours notice to sail for Greece. He visited an Egyptian photographic studio, had his photo taken, paid him in advance and asked that two copies be sent to his mother, with no great confidence that she would get them. She did.

Anthony Eden, Brittain's Foreign Minister at the time, visits Julis Camp, Palestine, 1940, where Charles trained.

"D" Company, from the 2/4th Battalion, on parade at Julis Camp, Palestine, 1940.

Sketch depicting an incident in the Battle of Tobruk,
in which Charles took part, 21 January, 1941.

Painting by Charles's second wife, Wendy, depicting his mate
"Rusty" McWilliam, triumphantly "raising the flag" by hoisting up
a slouch hat in the main square of Tobruk on 22 January, 1941.

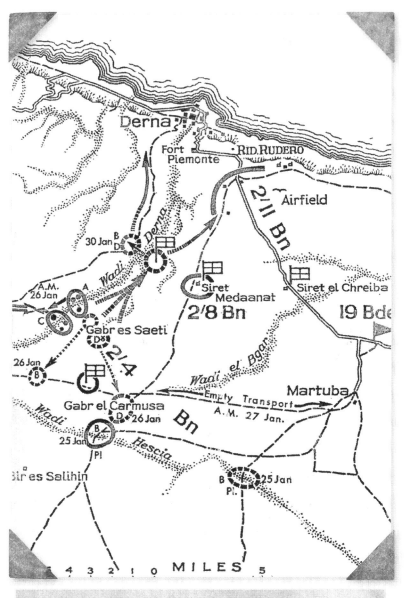

Battle map of the operation at Derna 25/26 January, 1941, where Charles fired his "first shot in anger".

Fraternising with the Greek people, Omonia Square, Athens,
April 1941. Australian War Memorial Neg No. 007528.
Charles experienced similar Greek hospitality.

Leave party at the Acropolis, Athens, 4 April, 1941,
Australian War Memorial Neg No. 006787.

Lt. Col. Dougherty (right) with Greek Commanding Officer Vevi near Monastir, 10 April, 1941. Lt. Col. Dougherty was Commander of the 2/4th Battalion at the time. Australia War Memorial, Neg No. 128423.

Infantry School of Signals, Nathanya, Palestine,
September, 1941 where Charles completed his NCO
training. Charles in the top row, second from right.

Sketch depicting a Bren carrier in action, Tobruk, 1941

Sketch depicting a battalion going through the wire, Tobuk, 1941

Stalag, 1943 - Kim Williams, Hec Virgona,
Joe Wishart, Ernie Wolfe and Charles.

Winter at Hermagor, 1943. Charles fifth in from the left, and Joe Wishart next to him in the cap.

Hermagor in the late winter of 1943. Charles on the far left, and Joe Wishart and Ernie Wolfe, second and third in from the right respectively.

The Pilgrimage Church of the Assumption of Mary on Bled Island,
which was spotted by Charles, Jack Wooster and Ray Teitjen, as they
hid in the hills after an escape attempt from Hermagor in 1944.

Längsee

The castle at St. Georgen, where Charles spent time in his final disciplinare camp in 1945. Charles worked on converting the castle into a military hospital.

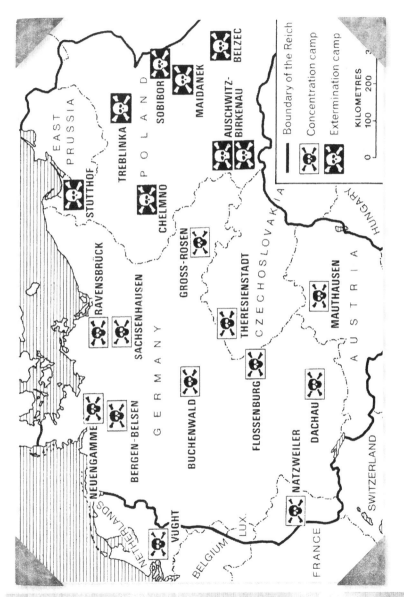

The bleak deathsheads map of Nazi camps, including Theresienstadt, where New Zealanders such as Tom Mottram and Gerald Mills were held, and where other New Zealanders were allegedly executed for refusing to work. *Tom Mottram Collection.*

The mostly one-way Long March prisoners of war were required
by the Germans to make away from the advancing Russians.
Redrawn from Official History of New Zealand in the Second
World War, volume on "Prisoner of War". *Tom Mottram Collection.*

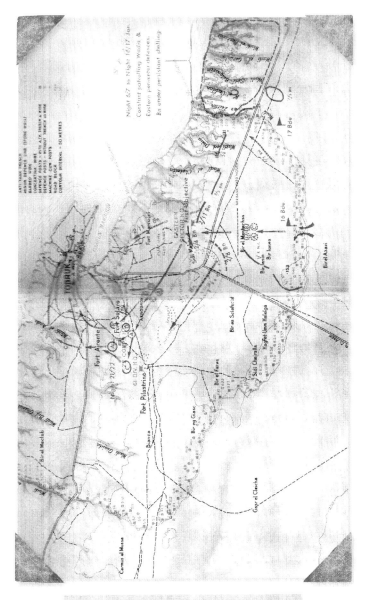

Map of operations, Tobruk, January, 1941.

Photograph of Jack "Lofty" Barker taken in St Veit, 1945, after Germany surrendered.

Charles with his soon to be wife, Ann, taken in St. Veit after the war in June, 1945, where he was working disarming the Germans.

Ann and her friend Little Irena on her right, taken in St. Veit in June, 1945, before Irena was taken away and murdered by the Russians.

Cross roads near Xinon Neron, with Lake Petron in the background, 1960. The enclosed monument was erected by the Greeks in memory of men from the author's battalion killed in action on 12 April, 1941.

Charles revisiting Brallos Pass, Greece in 1994.
Returning to where he was wounded in 1941.

Brallos Pass from a painting by William Dargie,
Australian War Memorial, Neg. No. ART 26298.

Charles's wife, Wendy, in the woods of Daphni, Greece, 1994.
Revisiting the woods where Charles's battalion had camped in 1941.

By the KING'S Order the name of
Sergeant C. R. Granquist,
Australian Military Forces,
was published in the London Gazette on
23 January, 1947,
as mentioned in a Despatch for distinguished service.
I am charged to record
His Majesty's high appreciation.

Secretary of State for War

Charles Granquist's Mention in Despatches Citation.

not the place to get fat. Each morning we got a bread roll and a mug of coffee. At midday it was a bowl of soup or stew. In the evening we had to make do with another cup of coffee. Belts and bootlaces were confiscated along with any knives or other implements that we might use to do ourselves in. Every day we were given one hour in the exercise yard. Generally we just walked in circles holding on to our trousers.

Once a week we were shaved by a lifer with a cut-throat razor – one of the more nerve-wracking experiences we encountered. The cell had two double bunks and a toilet and small wash basin in one corner. There were no table or chairs and the only place to sit was on your bunk. The Englishman regaled us constantly with explicit details of his many sexual adventures. Old Bill, who was pretty straight up and down, didn't hack this very well at all. I found some of it quite interesting but after a while it got a bit too much. How someone on short rations could spend so much time thinking about sex beat me. It was a feature of POW life that, when rations were short, conversation was always about a big steak and eggs or similar; but at times when the food supply improved, the talk was about women.

After our month in the hands of the Italians, two German guards arrived and marched us down to Udine station where we boarded a train for Germany. Eventually we were back in Stalag 18A at Wolfsberg where we were sentenced to 28 days of solitary confinement plus bread and water. This meant three days bread and water and one day full rations (bread, a bowl of soup and a cup of ersatz coffee). The cell was high and narrow with a very small window high up on the back wall so it was impossible to look out.

I suffered from claustrophobia but suffered just one nasty episode. I awoke from a deep sleep to find the cell was pitch black and it took me ages to find the light at the small window. That feeling of terror relates back to an incident growing up on our farm. I was playing in a big trunk belonging to my father when I realised I couldn't get out. Panic-stricken, I hammered on it until my mother heard me.

We had one hour's exercise each day and were allowed one shower a week. On being released from solitary we received a Red Cross parcel which was wonderful after a long time without much in the way of decent food. Not long after we got out old Bill was sent to a working camp and I never saw him again. He made it home eventually and after the war I was delighted to catch up with him over the phone when he called me from Victoria.

Back in the camp's general population I met up with three Australians – Hec Virgona, Ernie Wolfe and Joe Wishart. Although from time to time we were separated we remained the very best of mates during the war and after.

The Germans made it known that any future escapees or other transgressors would, after interrogation, be sent to a disciplinaire camp where work would be harder and security stricter. The camps were set up to deter escapees but in fact they had the reverse effect because they clumped together all the recalcitrants in a centre of intrigue and scheming. It was precisely the wrong the thing our captors could have done.

Our desire to escape caused a division between disciplinaires and those who behaved themselves. I never had a problem with those who decided to see the war out as quietly and safely as possible, but there were isolated instances where we were accused of buggering things up for everybody by making the Germans stricter and less friendly. However, I was unrepentant. I just wanted to get home and thought my way was the best way to do that.

Joe Wishart had a marvellous tenor voice. One day an accordion from the Red Cross arrived and almost every night he would sing popular pre-war songs for us to enjoy. This raised our morale considerably. Around this time we were shocked by an incident of stealing, which was very unusual in POW camps. The following poem, with apologies to the Scarlet Pimpernel, did the rounds:

"They seek him here
They seek him there
Those prisoners seek him everywhere
Does he live in this?
Does he live in that?
That damned elusive Wolfsberg cat

The ghostly hour of midnight knells
And stealthy pawsteps creep
Into that dingy hell of hells
Where muttering prisoners sleep

This silent, cunning feline thief
Has early found the knack
Of opening tins of bully beef
That clutter up his track

This dangerously active crook and toff
So inside rumours say

Suffers from a smoker's cough
As well we think he may

One day his ardent love of fags
Will lead him to a trap
And then he'll walk around in rags
When he's finished off his rap"

The Germans insisted that anyone caught stealing be handed over to them for punishment but we certainly would not have done this. In the German Army, any stealing, irrespective of the value, was punishable by a stint in a military prison, which we knew to be most unpleasant. The offender was never caught but the stealing stopped. Perhaps he had been sent to a working camp.

The reason that I was still at Wolfsberg soon became apparent. All non-commissioned officers were soon to be sent to a camp in Poland and did not have to work. The same thing would apply to German NCOs in British hands. This was dreadful news to me. I was determined to attempt another escape and the opportunities in the very south of Germany were much more attractive than in Poland. After all, what could you do if you were stuck in Poland? Try to swim to Sweden? On top of this I would be separated from my mates. The solution came from an unexpected source.

I crossed paths with an Englishman by the name of Trooper Frederick Harvey from the 11th Hussars. I wanted to stay with my mates, the privates. He said: "That's fine". He was so keen to avoid work he was prepared to change identity with me. All we had to do was exchange our German dog tags and off he went to Poland. I don't know if this was a common occurrence but I certainly never heard of anyone else doing this. I thought it was a godsend. I certainly never had any fears about what it might mean for my family had anything happened to Harvey. When I lost my discharge papers in the 1980s I called army records to get a new copy. I had been debriefed after the war about my experiences, including the identity switch. The bloke I spoke to at the records office in Melbourne was fascinated and rang me later to find out more about why I did it and how.

It was generally believed that the NCOs were going to Stalag XXA in Poland, although a similar camp, Stalag 383, was established at Hohenfels in central Germany later in 1942. But Frederick had long gone by then so I thought he had gone to Thorn. If they had kept him there he would have been stuck in that dreadful winter march from Thorn to Fallingbostel in 1945. Wherever he was, he would be facing years of the most soul-destroying boredom, while I could continue my escape attempts with not much time to be bored.

I went to a camp close to Wolfsberg – a paper mill at a place called Frantschach. On arrival we had to give our names, which was quite unusual. When they came to me the guard barked "name" and I started to say "Granquist" before quickly changing to "Harvey". He turned to his offsider and said, "This stupid Englander doesn't even know his own name". Little did he know!

Frantschach was not a disciplinaire camp. The work at the paper mill was hard but the food was fairly good. If you wanted to see out the war while behaving yourself then it was probably not a bad place to do so. However, Yugoslavia beckoned. The border was only a few days' march away and there was a lot of talk of British submarines sneaking into the Dalmatian coast with supplies for the partisans. I started planning an escape to Yugoslavia and onto the coast with another Australian bloke, whose name I forget (probably because I wanted to). This escape was very poorly planned. It was put together in a hurry and with insufficient thought given to my escape companion. However, the weather was nice and warm and the escape bug was biting hard, so commonsense did not prevail. We again cut the wire when the guard was around the back of the camp and headed off into the hills where we found a track heading south and followed this for two nights. There were several shelter huts on the track and this is where my companion, we'll call him Bill, and I first fell out. He wanted to – and did – sleep in the huts. I believed it was safer to sleep in the woods.

Comfort didn't come into it. Bill got more and more bad-tempered and eventually decided he was going to part company with me and go it alone. I didn't cross paths with him again but heard later that a couple of policemen had caught him sleeping in a hut. I kept going south for another two nights and was just about on the Yugoslav border when I walked into a German patrol.

I saw them but the worst thing you could do was run because you'll get shot. The scariest part of this escaping caper was the point of re-capture. Staring down the barrels of a number of rifles and wondering whether some nervous and trigger-happy German might tighten his finger was, to say the very least, discomforting. However, this lot was quite OK and obviously had been warned that there were a couple of escapees to look out for. Back at their headquarters they made sure they did indeed have an Englander "kriegsgefanger" (prisoner of war) and actually gave me something to eat.

The new punishment regime for disciplinaires had now come into force and I was taken by a long train journey to Landeck in the Tyrol. This was an interrogation camp, ironically in sight of the Swiss border, high up in the mountains still covered in snow. There followed about two weeks of solitary confinement and daily questioning by an English-speaking German officer. He was obviously trying to find out whether I had any help from civilians or whether any sabotage was planned. What I was able to tell him could have been covered in one session but he kept at it.

There were other POWs in a number of cells but all contact with them was forbidden. Eventually, we were taken out, bundled into a train and taken on another lengthy journey to Markt Pongau prison camp. Markt Pongau was an absolute bitch of a place that was clearly intended to soften us up and make us regret the error of our ways. It was lousy with fleas and great big bed bugs which emerged at night and bit the hell out of you. All the beds had charred bedposts where previous occupants had burned off the bedbugs in an attempt to kill some of them off. Decent sleep was impossible. The guards must have been specially selected. They were a bad-tempered lot and if you looked sideways at one you were very likely to cop a rifle butt.

After about a week in this holiday resort I was sent back to the Stalag at Wolfsberg for another 28 days of bread and water. On release, another Red Cross parcel and some cigarettes made life seem almost rosy. I was very pleased to pick up with Joe Wishart again but Ernie and Hec had been sent out to working camps.

The problem of telling my mother about my new name was overcome by devious means using the cards we were allowed to write home. Mum had two nieces in England who worked in a tobacco factory and arranged for them to send me parcels of cigarettes. Of course, Frederick in Poland was now getting these. No one seemed to love him as I didn't even get any letters addressed to him. It was a long time before the changeover of identity was finally foolproof.

Joe and I were then sent on to another disciplinaire camp where we were put to work in a magnesite quarry. It was hard-going and the guards were quite touchy. One day a New Zealander told one of the guards to "get fucked" and got shot and badly wounded for his trouble. The food was poor but we did get some Red Cross parcels which allowed us to squirrel away some supplies for another escape attempt before winter closed in.

The barbed wire was quite close to the side of the hut so we took up the floorboards under Joe's bed and began digging a tunnel. The plan was to come out a short distance outside the wire where there were some bushes. We put the spoil up in the ceiling. One day a guard had a look up there and we thought we were goners. Incredibly, he assumed someone had been growing mushrooms. We couldn't believe our luck. Everybody helped and we took a few bedboards from each bed to shore up the walls and roof. Disciplinaires were now a close-knit group of men and there was a wonderful spirit among us. The majority were Australians and New Zealanders but there were some notable British exceptions.

When the tunnel was finished Joe and I crawled through, pushing our packs in front of us. Before breaking out we waited for those inside the hut to tell us that the guard was around the other side. We climbed out, soil and roots hanging off us, and ran for our lives. My claustrophobia really started to hit in that tunnel even though it was short.

Our plan was to pass through Hungary, Bulgaria and Macedonia into Turkey. We set course in the general direction of Vienna, intending to skirt around the city until we found a bridge over the Danube from where we would head to Hungary. The second night out it started to rain quite heavily and we got soaked. Joe was not feeling at all well and we decided to forego a night's march and found a barn to sleep in where we could dry our clothes out and get some decent rest. We had to get out of the barn before daylight and headed for the woods for the usual rest-up. It was still raining like buggery and Joe was feeling worse. "Look, I really can't go on," he said. "I'm holding you up. I'll give myself up."

He gave me some of his food and it was agreed that he would wait as long as possible before handing himself in. He was to tell Jerry that we had gone our separate ways after escaping, but it was doubtful that this story would be believed and an alert would almost certainly be issued.

That night it continued to rain. It was very dark and progress was slow but just before daylight the rain eased and I found a spot up in the hills where I dried out and had a good sleep. Good progress was made during the next four nights. Then, from where I was in the hills, I sighted Vienna. It was much more spread out than I expected and skirting round the southern side looked like being a long journey.

Eventually I got into open country, turned east and began making good time on a rural road when I came round a corner and into the arms of two policemen. I was handcuffed and taken back to the station. In the morning they moved me to Vienna where, after some waiting around, I was handed over to an army guard. After travelling for two days in handcuffs, I arrived at Feldkirchen which was an interrogation centre just kilometres away from the Swiss border. I had always wanted to see Vienna, the city of Strauss, but not in handcuffs through a train window. After about two weeks at Feldkirchen it was off to, joy of joys, Markt Pongau.

After fighting off the fleas and bed bugs, which seemed to have grown bigger in my absence, it was back to Wolfsberg and the usual 28 days of bread and water.

Chapter 9 - On The Run Again

CHAPTER 10

A DIFFERENT CRIME

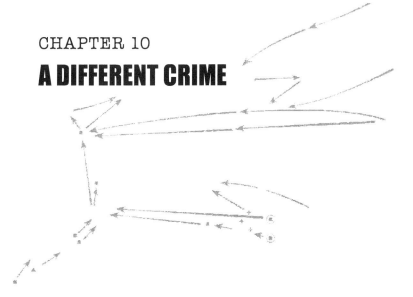

By now I was an old lag and knew quite a few lurks to make life in the bunker more tolerable. Fulfilling the desire for a smoke was near the top of the list. Thankfully, while taking my daily walk in the exercise yard, my mates outside would often throw me some cigarettes when the guards weren't looking. You still had to light them and one ingenious character came up with a way: Scrape some fine shavings off a celluloid toothbrush handle with a safety razor blade, and then scrape the blade on a smuggled flint until a spark fell on the shavings which ignited easily. You had to smoke as close as possible to the small window. It was quite satisfying, but it didn't do the razor blade any good.

As long as the POWs received regular Red Cross parcels, life in the main camp was quite tolerable. A concert party was formed and put on some good shows that were even attended by some of the German guards. They seemed to enjoy the performances despite primarily being there to make sure there were no skits on poking fun at the Führer, or for that matter at anything German.

There were several radios secreted around the camp and it really was uplifting to hear Big Ben strike seven before the announcement: "This is the overseas service of the BBC." At that time the German 6th Army was engaged in a tremendous struggle to capture Stalingrad. They expected it to fall at any time and believed that would mean the end of the war in Russia. The BBC told us otherwise, providing details of the Soviet forces' heroic resistance. We also knew the Afrika Corps had been defeated at El Alamein. It seemed, at last, that the tide of the war was turning our way. This new wave of optimism brought a catch-cry, often heard at night, of: "When will they come?" It also produced the following poem:

"We ask, and in our plaintive voices cry,
When will they come? Oh when, oh when?
And answering echoes in their passing by,
Say patience, patience, until then.

And nightly when the tempests rage and roar,
We appeal with voices both of hope and fear,
To God, prayer in our hearts, expectant evermore,
That he may say, be at rest! For they are here!"

One day we were all turned out of our huts and made to stand on the parade ground while the Gestapo searched the camp for radios and escape material such as maps and civilian clothing. After about three hours they triumphantly appeared carrying one wireless set and a few civilian clothes which were, in fact, the property of the concert party. No doubt they tore strips off the Commandant for such negligence and then departed. The Commandant was Hauptman (Captain) Steiner, an officer who had served in World War I, and was respected by the prisoners as a fair man. He had an awful bark but his bite was rather gentle. In fact, during the last few days of the war the whole camp was moved westwards to Markt Pongau ahead of the advancing Russians. As a result the POWs made a request to the British occupying force that the Hauptman be sent to his home by car. This they did.

But that was still in the future. I was sent to a disciplinaire camp at Leoben in Steirmark in Eastern Austria. It was a railway town and we were all working on different jobs connected with the railway. A gang of us was sent out to replace worn and rotted sleepers on the permanent way. The foreman marked the sleepers to be replaced before we dug out all the blue metal, dragged out the sleepers, put in new ones and repacked the metal. The foreman checked it and then drove in the spikes.

It was tiresome work but Jerry didn't drive us too hard. From there we were set to work strengthening a bridge so that it was capable of taking the weight of trains carrying tanks and guns. These were destined for the Russian front and we didn't feel good about it. But we had no option and disappointingly there was no opportunity for sabotage. Work was carried out on a swinging stage over the river. We had to chip the paint off all the existing joints before a civilian welded in some triangular shaped pieces of metal. After that we had to prime the whole area with a red lead primer. A passenger train took us to and from work and by the time we clambered aboard to go back to camp it was getting dark. We were ordered to stand in the corridor, which had a guard stationed at each end. As the female conductor passed through she had to squeeze by all the prisoners. On the way she received quite a bit of attention but didn't seem to mind. It seemed that German women had begun to notice the absence of young, able-bodied men and were starting to become attracted to British POWs. However, the penalty for consorting with one was severe. Usually, the prisoner was sent to a military prison and the woman's hair was shaved off before she was paraded through the streets of her village or town carrying a placard declaring her to be a traitor to the Reich. And then she was thrown into jail.

As disciplinaires, we had very little contact with women. It was a different matter for some of the well-behaved POWs, particularly those who worked on farms. The guard would deliver the POW to the farm in the morning and pick him up at night. The old man was, of course, away on the Russian front fighting his little heart out for his Führer, so it was open slather. Sometimes it made us reflect that perhaps crime didn't pay.

Each camp had a Vertraunsman or "man of confidence", essentially the go-between POWs and their German jailers. I was elected to this post and soon found that it came with drawbacks. The Germans blasphemed badly but never used swear words with a sexual connotation. Unfortunately, they quickly learnt what our swear words meant. Sometimes a prisoner in trouble with a guard would tell me to "tell him to go and get fucked". You could warn him of the consequences, but if he was really angry he'd reply: "Go on, tell him". You would convey this as well as you could. The guard would usually go ballistic and occasionally hit you instead of the prisoner. After learning the hard way, my advice inevitably became: "If you want to tell him that, you tell him yourself".

It was getting close to Christmas of 1942 when we began brewing a concoction called "fong". The basic recipe involved collecting all the windfall apples and pears you could find, putting them in a metal dish along with any raisins left over from Red Cross parcels, placing another dish on top and allowing the lot to ferment. Sometimes we added potato peelings. After it had fermented we put a copper pipe (stolen from the engine shed) between the dishes so that the brew could drip into a container. Then we put the whole lot on the stove, brought the liquid to a boil, before packing snow around the pipe. The steam condensed, leaving us with a drink that boasted a powerful kick.

We started on the fong on Christmas Eve. "Weinachten" is traditionally a time of great celebration for Germans. The guards were getting stuck into it and didn't seem too concerned about security. About a dozen of us, in an alcoholic haze, decided to leave camp and go into the town. We agreed that no one would turn this excursion into an escape attempt before cutting the wire and heading off. I knew where our foreman lived and made a beeline for his house. He and his wife invited me in and gave me schnapps and a special biscuit. We talked for quite a while. After taking my leave I tried to find the others but by now the guards and the police were out in force. I staggered back to camp and handed myself in. We avoided being punished for this escapade after I explained to the Commandant that it was all done in the spirit of Christmas and we had no intention of escaping. Nevertheless the Commandant, who wasn't a bad bloke, was sent off to the Russian front and I was no longer a "man of confidence".

Early one morning we awoke to a terrific roar and thought at first that it must be an Allied air raid. It turned out to be a big avalanche which had thundered down a nearby mountain, bringing trees and rocks with it and blocking the railway line for almost a kilometre. We were pitchforked out of bed and sent there on a train. We had to shovel the snow into the train's trucks so it could be taken away and dumped into the river. Another crew of civilians worked away from the other side. It took several days of around-the-clock labouring to clear the line.

It was around this time that I was called to the Commandant's office and told that Frederick Harvey had spilt the beans in Poland. I was to be sent to the Stalag at Wolfsberg for punishment. Leaving Leoben and my mate Hec Virgona was quite a blow as we had some carefully prepared plans for the spring. Hec's parents, who owned Geelong's ABC café and restaurant (one of the city's premier eating houses), were Italian and he was fluent in the language. Hec taught me the intricacies of bridge and in due course we played very well together.

As I waited to be transported back to Stalag to do my time I was sent out each day to dig out a hole for a swimming pool for officers at a nearby army camp. My guard was a Gefreiter (Corporal) called Hans who was convalescing after being badly wounded at Stalingrad. We got on so well that he used to stand at the top of the hole and warn me if anybody was coming so I could pretend to look busy.

Hans had served in the 44th Austrian Division of the ill-fated 6th Army and told me how he and his comrades had pushed out of the Ukraine, captured Kharkov and Voronezh and driven through to Stalingrad. They had believed they were well on the way to winning the war in Russia. Hitler was even moved to say that "with the 6th Army he could storm the heavens". But, once in Stalingrad, the wheels started to fall off.

Hans' division was in the northern sector when the Russians launched a massive attack in early January 1943. His division was virtually destroyed and he was badly wounded. Miraculously he was taken to the airfield and evacuated in one of the last transports to leave Stalingrad. When he heard of the surrender at Stalingrad he realised that Germany could not win the war and it had opened his eyes to the fact that

Hitler was a terrible leader to have allowed it to happen. He assumed that he'd be sent back to the Russian front when his wounds healed. I don't know what happened to him but I hope he survived. Although he was my guard, and I his prisoner, we seemed to be equals – just two infantry soldiers trying their best to get through the war.

Back at Wolfsberg, my identity was restored together with the usual naughty boy's diet of 28 days bread and water, or "brot und wasser". I now knew most of the "crims" who had been recycled through the system and we made a point of comparing notes during our one-hour exercise sessions. Several disciplinaires carried on their own relentless war against the Germans. Blokes like Eric Black, a cheeky young bloke from Sydney, who could not resist having a go at the guards if he was displeased about something. One day he stretched the elastic too far and was shot dead in an altercation. "Pluto" Giessen was another incorrigible. On one occasion he caused so much trouble in jail that they suspended him by his thumbs with his toes just touching the floor until he agreed to behave himself.

For some reason I was left in the Stalag for a longer than normal time before being sent to a disciplinaire "lager" and rather enjoyed the break. The cookhouse food was much the same but the regular Red Cross parcels and cigarette issues made life a lot more tolerable. Mum and Mary must have wondered what the hell was going on when I started writing to them in my own name again. It was a long time before the change back to my real identity was complete. In all that time nothing had come my way in the name of Trooper Frederick Harvey. It was no consolation that he had done all right out of it.

An English sergeant who was on Wolfsberg camp staff devised a clever escape plan. He managed to get his hands on a good set of civilian clothes complete with a Tyrolean hat as worn by nearly all the locals. A number of civilians worked in the camp. One day he mounted a stolen pushbike and tacked on the back of the group as it left to go home. The main gate opened and away he went. Pedaling through the village of Wolfsberg he slipped on an icy section of road and fell heavily. Several civilians rushed to help and, as he couldn't speak much German, held him until the police arrived. In no time at all he was back in the Stalag.

At least the war news was getting better and better. We knew that the German 6th Army had surrendered at Stalingrad and up to 200,000 had been captured. It was payback time for the Russians. It's been well-documented that after the war fewer than 6,000 of the poor buggers saw their homes again.

Thanks to the Geneva Conventions we were a lot better off. Life in Stalag went on as usual, brightened by the war news but tempered by the knowledge that the German Army was by no means beaten and we had a fair while to go yet. We were also hearing that the tide had turned against the Japs in the Pacific but were unaware of the cruel and barbaric treatment handed out to our POWs.

Early in the spring of '43 I was sent to a disciplinaire camp at Hermagor where I was delighted to meet up again with Ernie Wolfe and Joe Wishart. Hec Virgona was in another camp only a few kilometres up the line. My new job was in a blue metal quarry. Every POW had to fill eight skips with blue metal rocks each day and wheel them down to the crusher. You were given a metal disc in exchange for a load. Your work was finished when you handed in your eight discs. Sunday was our only day off. Some of the stronger prisoners worked by themselves, but most of us worked in pairs loading 16 skips per day.

We were paid for our labours – a measly 70 pfennigs (pence) a day. This magnificent sum bought very little of any use. We could purchase matches and cigarette papers, but no cigarettes or tobacco. The only useful item available was toilet paper. Our paper money was regarded with such disdain that poker players refused to play with it. Cigarettes were the only "legal" tender. After the war the British Government honoured the currency and exchanged it at the official rate. Once again the real smarties cashed in by taking a pack full of the stuff back to England and exchanging it for Sterling.

The quarry was owned by Herr Brass, a typically rotund German, who inspired a song which we delighted in singing to the tune of the Communist Internationale:

"We'll wave the scarlet banner high,
Beneath its shades we'll live and die,
And Mr Brass can kiss my arse,
I've got a bludger's job at last."

My bludger's job was wielding the pneumatic drill which was marginally better than filling skips. Admittedly you did not have the pressure of filling those eight a day but by the time your work was finished your teeth were chattering and you were covered with stone dust.

Inevitably, tempters frayed and I remember one Australian bloke telling a guard to "go and get fucked". I could speak rough German so I had to accompany him to Villach to front the Area Commander. The Hauptman asked the guard what the prisoner said and he snapped to attention and barked: "Herr Hauptman er sagt fucky fucky". The prisoner's sentence was a foregone conclusion – 28 days of "brot und wasser". It meant a nice day off for me.

The war news was rapidly improving. We knew, courtesy of men arriving from the Stalag, that the Germans had suffered a major defeat at Kursk and lost a lot of their armour on the Russian Front. Also, German forces in North Africa had surrendered and the Allies had landed on Sicily. Things were looking good.

Chapter 10 - A Different Crime

CHAPTER 11
HERE WE GO AGAIN

My bludger's job on the pneumatic drill was over and I was back on the skips again which didn't seem so bad after my time drilling the quarry face with metre-long bits that had a knack of getting stuck. My mate on the skips was Jack "Lofty" Barker, a New Zealander, and we worked very well together.

Jack was an anti-tank gunner and had already proved to be one tough bloke. On the 19th of April 1941 near Mount Olympus he copped a machine gun bullet through the groin. He was evacuated to hospital in Athens before being taken prisoner. He received quite good medical treatment but was discharged before recovering fully. After a short stop at the large POW holding camp at Corinth, Jack joined a group being taken to Salonika in northern Greece and then to Germany. The prisoners travelled by train to the southern side of the Brallos Pass, but because all the bridges had been blown they were forced to march over the pass to Lamia, about 25 miles away. Jack had to make the march in hospital-issue carpet slippers and by the time he got to Salonika he felt so bad he feared he would die. The day after arriving in Salonika the Germans wanted everybody on parade for a headcount. Jack ignored the call, prompting two German soldiers to grab him by the feet, drag him onto the parade ground with his head bumping on the ground and dump him in line. When the parade was over he heard someone laughing. Despite his dazed state he recognised the laugh as belonging to his mate Cyril Crooks. Cyril and a couple of others helped Jack to the hut where they nursed him back to health. He still had the horror train trip from Salonika to Austria to go but he made it. Tough bloke our Jack!

There were about 30 of us in the camp and they were a great mob of blokes except for a Pacific Islander called Bill. He was an enormously strong man who always finished his work before us. He often hung around the Commandant and any off duty guards who virtually gave him the run of the place. We made sure that any escape talk didn't take place when he was about as we felt sure that he would inform the Germans.

Our "man of confidence" at the time was Jack Wooster, a New Zealander, and a man of very strong character. Bill could have flattened him with one swipe of his massive hand but Jack kept at him about his traitorous conduct without success. In the end he told Bill that he would charge him after the war. Bill just laughed at him, saying the Germans were going to win the war anyway. As I understand it, he was court martialled in New Zealand after the war and received a jail sentence.

Towards the end of summer there were strong rumours that the Italians were going to toss it in and the idea of being in Italy when they capitulated seemed to offer great possibilities. Our Italian-speaking mate, Hec Virgona, was an important factor in our plans. I can't remember how we communicated with him, but we somehow did enough for him to agree to go when we were ready. Ernie Wolfe and Joe Wishart were to go first. I was to meet up with Hec and follow them.

We had trouble getting started. Firstly, Ernie and Joe's escape gear was discovered by a civilian, possibly after a tip-off from Bill. When they got back to camp after serving time in the bunker we decided to go as soon as possible. They got some gear together in a hurry but the escape was put on hold again when news came from Hec that he would be delayed another couple of days. We decided to go anyway and that I would hide out in an old disused shack above the quarry till he was ready. I was there for two days and nights, scared stiff all the time that I would be sprung. Thankfully I had help from Dolly Grey, an English POW, who was a poacher from Kings Lynne and could move like a fox. He would wait for an opportunity to shoot up the side of the quarry to the hut to bring me some food and any news of Hec. Good old Dolly, bless him, eventually brought word that Hec would be breaking out that night and I was to meet him on the near side of the bridge that crossed the river about a kilometre down the line. I set out after dark and, sure enough, there was Hec waiting for me. We crossed the bridge and headed south to the Italian Alps.

The next day we hid out high in the hills above the camp from where we could see any search parties coming across the valley. We could well imagine the hoo-ha that was going on. We took turns sleeping and watching but were left in peace. That night we pushed on until reaching a little church which we knew was very near the Italian border. After resting during the day we set out again the next night, following a dirt road till we came to what was obviously the border. There were no frontier posts to worry about so we walked over and kept to the same road for the rest of the night. The next day we kept on going, stopping only for a rest and a brew, not caring whether we were seen or not. Not long after we set off again we spotted a group of Italian soldiers and gave ourselves up.

Hec told them that the war for Italy was almost "finito" and they would do well to point us in the direction of the partisans. Whether they knew or not, they were too frightened of the Germans to do anything else but take us to headquarters. The same conversation took place there with the same result and we were bundled off to my old "alma mater", Udine prison.

In Udine who should we meet but Ernie and Joe. They took the same escape route we did and suffered the same fate, crossing paths with an Italian patrol. It was a Sunday and the soldiers at the Italian barracks wanted to go to Mass. Their two Protestant prisoners had no choice but to join them. Thanks to Hec's powers of persuasion we ended up together in a cell. The same old Italian lags were still there, including the lifer with his cutthroat razor. The food was still as sumptuous as before as we settled down to wait for the Italian surrender. Hec sought and was granted an interview with the Governor of the jail. He told him that he would guarantee that Churchill would pay the Governor a bonus of 1,000 pounds if he released us when Italy tossed it in. The governor seemed quite attracted to the first part of the proposition but this was trumped by his fear of what the local Germans might do if he let us go. We were unaware that Hec had contact with Churchill but it was worth a try. There were no other POWs in the jail but Hec was able to talk to the other lags and keep us up to date with prison news. At night the prisoners talked to each other by tapping on the pipes which ran up the inside of the cell walls. It was a code that was impossible to decipher.

As time passed we presumed that a surrender must be very close. Hec, obviously after consulting Churchill again, sought another interview with the Governor. He offered to increase the reward but was knocked back. We had no other option but to settle down and wait. Eventually two German guards came to collect us. The four of us were handcuffed, taken to Udine station and put on a train back to Deutschland. It was one of those typical German autumn mornings – a heavy mist hung in the air just like rain. We changed trains at Villach and to compound our misery we learned that the Italians had capitulated. It was the 3rd of September. Just one bloody day too late for us!

Four very dejected POWs arrived back at Wolfsberg to start another 28 days' solitary on bread and water. At least we were used to it. Life in the camp continued as usual but the war news was encouraging. Hearing that the Japanese were very much on the back foot and that Australia was safe from invasion was a great morale boost. This was very important to us as we now knew first-hand what happened when countries were occupied by a barbaric invader. Germany was full of millions of slave labourers from just about every country in Europe and Russia and we still weren't aware of Hitler's Final Solution. Compared to those poor people, we had it good.

The surrounding hills were ablaze with the colours of autumn. It was a beautiful sight but we knew that another grim winter was ahead of us. Some of the supreme optimists thought it might be the last one but it didn't seem likely considering France had not yet been invaded. One day a German soldier came up to the compound gate and started to talk to some of our blokes. They were shocked to learn he was an Englishman from the Stalag who had changed sides and joined the British Free Korps. Why on earth anybody in their right mind would become a traitor is impossible to fathom, especially when Blind Freddy could see the Germans were going to lose the war. Who knows what happened to him. Perhaps he ended up spreadeagled in the snow on the Russian Front because that was where most of the foreign volunteers were sent.

Joe finally had his piano accordion again and he was almost exhausted by the sheer number of requests to sing all the old numbers. There was a fellow in camp called Bob Oliver who was a marvellous musician and wrote many songs. The following, *Roll On The Boat*, was very popular:

"What are we thinking of
What are we dreaming of, dreaming all day long
What are we hoping for, what are we hoping for
Listen to my song –

Roll on the boat, the boat that takes me back to Blighty
Roll on the boat, the boat that takes me home to you
Deutschland goodbye, we'll soon see Blighty's shore
So roll on the boat, the boat that takes me home to you."

The following song *Exile*, with music by Bob Oliver and lyrics by Cec Johnson, is very sentimental. But we were rather a sentimental lot, even though most of us had no-one to be particularly sentimental about, apart from our families.

"The whisper of the Austrian pine trees
Sings me songs of you.
The beauty of the Austrian mountains
Breaks my heart anew.

Every star that shines, entwines
My aching heart with yours
Every flower reminds me of
The smile my heart adores.

The glory of the Austrian sunset,
Every golden hue,
Tells me I'm in lonely exile,
Far away from you.

But when the moonlight softly taps
Upon my window pane,
When midnight brings me sleep,
You're in my arms again."

All good things come to an end and I was soon drafted to another disciplinaire camp and, praise be, it was Hermagor again. Hec, Ernie and Joe were sent to other camps and I would not see them again until well after the war. Disciplinaire camps were normally small because of the limited number of POW candidates. Many of the German soldiers staffing the camps had been wounded in battle. Instead of being sent to convalescent hospitals they were posted to prison camps as guards. They knew what war was all about and on the whole they treated us pretty well.

I was very pleased to be back at Hermagor again (eight skips a day and all) because most of the old hands were still there, including Jack Wooster, still fighting his private war with Bill, the Pacific Islander. The winter of 1943-44 was quite severe, with a lot of snow. We lost quite a bit of time in the morning clearing the snow away from the work site and the cold took a toll on your hands. Sixteen skips a day between two men often meant we only finished after dark. However, it still was not a bad camp to winter in and, apart from Bill, they were a great group of blokes. The return to my real name, as far as Mum and Mary were concerned, had finally been achieved and I started to receive mail from Australia. They told me my battalion had been back for a long time and that Gary Hart had visited my mother. He gave her as much information as he could about what happened to me and she had been comforted by his visit.

My itchy feet came back with a vengeance when spring arrived. Yugoslavia beckoned with the possibility of getting through to the Dalmatian Coast or joining up with the partisans, who we knew were making things pretty unpleasant for the Germans. Jack Wooster, another New Zealander Ray Teitjen and I started to make plans and accumulate food for what we hoped would be a long trip. We decided to wait till late June when the weather would be nice and warm and make sleeping in the open more comfortable.

Chapter 11 - Here We Go Again

CHAPTER 12
THE LAST HURRAH

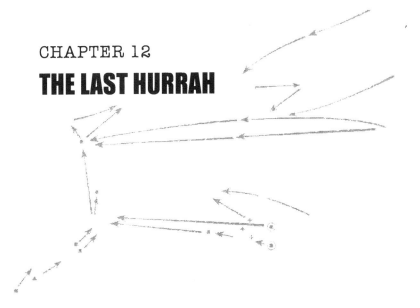

Late June arrived and the first part of our plan went off without a hitch. The wire was cut when the guard was around the other side. We bolted south, trying to go as far as possible before first light sent us unto the hills to find a suitable hiding place. Shortly after we left Hermagor we turned east to avoid crossing the Italian border. According to our map, we then had to go due south, following the Dinaric Alps, through Slovenia and Croatia to the Dalmatian coast. We intended to follow this right through, not only to avoid the Germans in the valleys but with the hope of meeting up with the partisans. Jack, Ray and I kept going for about three nights until we were confident we'd crossed into Slovenia.

I knew we had when I looked down on a most wonderful sight. It was Lake Bled in north-western Slovenia. In the centre of the lake was an island on which stood, I later learned, the Pilgrimage Church of the Assumption of Mary. Absolute magic! But it also made me wonder why some of the most beautiful countries in the world have suffered most from war and destruction.

We stayed in the mountains because we knew the valleys would be full of German troops. It made for slow progress. After a day spent sleeping in a deserted mill we decided to risk moving in daylight. Our reasoning was that Jerry would not venture into the hills and we might have a better chance of finding the partisans. We didn't know that the partisans we were most likely to meet were the royalist Chetniks led by Draza Mihailovic. They were more interested in stopping Marshal Tito gaining control of Yugoslavia after the war to the point of collaborating with the Germans. Any help from them would have been very unlikely. Initially the British Government recognised Mihailovic as the nominal head of the resistance; this followed their normal policy of leaning to anybody supporting royalty. However, in May 1944 they switched their support to Tito after realising that the arms they supplied to the Chetniks were mainly being used against their countrymen and not to fight the Germans.

We had not seen a soul during eight days in the mountains. One day we came to a small village of about six or seven houses that appeared to be deserted. We sat up in the hills above it for some time but it seemed devoid of life so we cautiously made our way down. The village was quite empty and eerie. We hunted around in the forlorn hope of finding some food before beating it back into the hills in case a German patrol came along. Some 12 days had passed since our escape from Hermagor. I estimated we had at least another five days to go before we reached the coast but there was one big problem – we were almost out of food. There was no choice but to go down into the valley fields that night to try and find some vegetables.

Three very nervous escapees trekked down to the flat where we came across a small hut with smoke rising from its chimney. We decided to try our luck. There were two peasants inside, living in the one room and obviously very poor. They couldn't understand a word of English or German so we mimed that we were hungry and needed something to eat. I think they thought we were a German patrol and quickly produced some milk but no food. Jack feared they might suspect we were on the run and that they would report us to the Germans, so we beat it back into the hills without rabbiting any fields. The next morning we ate the last of our food. The day after that we walked on empty stomachs. It was so frustrating. We had been out for 14 days, which was a pretty fair achievement, and we were slowly approaching our goal. However, hunger makes men do rash things. We decided to venture down into the valley again to and find another farmhouse and perhaps some friendly people who might have something for us to eat.

Looking down from the hills we noticed large house with a collection of outbuildings so decided to give it a crack. As we approached the house a couple of dogs started barking at us and a young woman and an old couple emerged. We tried speaking German which the young woman understood. We told her who we were and that we were hungry and desperately needed food. She spoke to the other two who very pleasantly sat us down at an outside table and produced bread, cheese and milk which we gratefully wolfed down. We hoped we'd hit the jackpot and these people were on our side. It didn't register that the young woman had disappeared until she suddenly walked around the corner of the house with three Jerry soldiers armed to the teeth. In our innocence we thought that all Yugoslavs would be on our side but that certainly wasn't the case. At least we got lumbered on full stomachs!

We were marched to the local German headquarters where we were questioned before two guards watched over us at the railway station as we waited a long time for a train. Our journey took us through Zagreb, the capital of Croatia, into Austria where I believe we changed trains at Klagenfurt. Our final destination was an interrogation camp at Feldkirchen. This time the interrogation was quite lengthy as the officer in charge probed us about whether we had met any partisans and where we were heading.

I told him a number of times that had we found the partisans I wouldn't be sitting in front of him at Feldkirchen. Eventually he gave up and we were sent packing back to the pleasure resort at Markt Pongau and then on to Wolfsberg for another serve of 28 days. I calculated that, including Feldkirchen, I had spent 196 days in solitary confinement. That plus time spent on the track (on the run) and twiddling my thumbs in Stalag probably reduced by more than nine months the amount of time I could have contributed to the German war effort. Although all five of my escape attempts had failed they had diverted a small amount of German manpower away from more other activities. That, along with similar efforts by all disciplinaires, served (if only in a small way) to have an adverse effect on the German war effort.

Disciplinaires regarded fellow POWs who chose to sit the war out as time servers even though we respected their right to do so. The morale of disciplinaires was enhanced by the knowledge that they had tried to continue carrying the war to the Germans in every way they could. Despite discomfort and punishment they avoided the boredom that so many time servers must have felt. And boredom must have been a real killer. Certainly, for me, engaging in "criminal" activities washed away a lot of the guilt that I felt about becoming a POW.

Chapter 12 - The Last Hurrah

CHAPTER 13
WINDING DOWN

Despite the German rail system being hammered on a daily basis by the Allied air forces, the Red Cross somehow managed to get some parcels to our camp. Cigarettes in particular were welcome after emerging from the slammer. The general mood of the POWs was buoyant; the Allies had landed at Normandy and the Russians were poised at the Vistula River for their final thrust to Berlin. There was a very real prospect that the next winter would be our last in captivity. Jack Wooster and Ray Teitjen were with me in Stalag and we spent quite some time reflecting on our foray into Yugoslavia. They were both wonderful blokes, especially Jack who was a man of great physical, mental and moral strength. By now I had decided that with the end of the war in sight another escape attempt would probably put me in unnecessary danger so I settled down like a good boy. An added disincentive was a German move to declare certain areas around cities and large towns "death zones" to discourage sabotage. Without maps showing where these zones were escaping would be a deadly game of Russian roulette. The penalty for being caught in a death zone was to be shot without trial.

I had feared that the Germans would send me up to the NCO's camp after Frederick Harvey dobbed me in but by this time they had more important things to worry about than transporting one prisoner all that way. Now the Russians were closing on that part of Europe. Mentally and physically tired by the previous three years, I had just settled down to the quiet life when in the autumn I was moved to a small disciplinaire camp at St Georgen.

It was customary for new arrivals to be told of any bludger's jobs that were available so that they could apply, regardless of whether they had any experience. The only documentation a POW owned was his identity tag so this scam was easy until, of course, he fronted up to work. There was a job going with the plumber. Fortunately my boss was a very outspoken anti-Nazi. He knew immediately I was no plumber but he didn't put me in and we forged a very good relationship.

There wouldn't have been any more than 25 prisoners in the camp, mainly Australians and Kiwis (plus a few Brits) and they were a great lot. All of us had given up the idea of escaping and there was a very relaxed atmosphere. Some of them had excellent voices and singing was popular. A couple of lines of one particular song, Glenn Miller's *I'm Stepping Out With A Memory Tonight*, has stuck with me ever since:

  "Then after dark in a hansom thru the park,
  While reminiscin' I'll be kissin' you."

Among them was New Zealander Cyril Crooks, an avowed Communist who was determined to travel to Russia when the war was over, and an Aussie who spoke such fluent German his captors refused to believe he was born in Australia.

As far as I was concerned the plumbing job was going fine, especially after the boss realised I was incapable of anything that required even elementary knowledge of the trade. Instead I was put on threading pipes with a stock and dies, and then sent up into roof cavities to lag the hot and cold water pipes with felt and hessian. The latter was a beaut job in winter with the hot water pipes making the space lovely and warm. While my boss didn't worry me, he suddenly had a lot to worry about. One day two members of the Gestapo, looking very menacing in their long leather coats, arrived and took him away. I have no knowledge of his ultimate fate and can only hope he survived the war. His departure meant the end of my job and I was soon put to work in the forest. Perhaps Jerry thought I would apply the same skill and energy to an axe and crosscut saw as I did to my plumbing!

The winter was a cold one with very heavy snow and we regularly had to dig a path from the door to get out of the hut in the morning. However, we were able to stay reasonably warm at night thanks to the forestry blokes bringing home dry wood from the job and a small coal issue. There was a pine tree in the forest called a "gummi", a piece of which would ignite as if soaked in petrol even when green and wet. It was very handy for getting the fire started. It was dark by 5.00pm but by then we were all in our hut and rustling up the evening meal. Our boots and trousers were then handed in and locked in a room until morning. Why the Germans took this precaution was hard to fathom as nobody in their right senses would consider escaping in the depths of winter. At night we huddled around the fire and sang the same sentimental love songs over and over again. Most of this was idle dreaming. After nearly five years away from home most of the girlfriends, and even some of the wives, had moved on to greener pastures. It was a long time for a young woman to wait, not knowing whether the man she was waiting for would return anything like the one who went away to war.

My girlfriend went her own way very early in the piece and married before the end of the war. This never concerned me because our relationship was not terribly serious.

I didn't mind that work in the forests was hard and cold. The war was fast coming to an end, a fact most of the Germans were all too aware of. A few die-hards still believed the Führer would lead them to victory but they had lost their grip on reality. The German offensive in the West had been defeated, the 8th British and the 5th US Armies were fighting their way through Northern Italy and the Russians had closed up to the Oder River for their assault on Berlin. The Allies began flying bombing missions from Northern Italy and it warmed your heart to see large formations of Flying Fortresses passing overhead to bomb targets deeper in the German heartland. Most days brought Mustangs and Lightnings buzzing around the railways looking for locomotives to shoot up with their cannons. This eventually forced the Germans to hide their bullet-riddled trains in tunnels during the day, bringing all rail traffic to a standstill.

As the Germans retreated out of Russia they gathered up most of the women and boys and sent them back to Germany to work as slave labour. One day about a dozen young Ukrainian women and three boys arrived to work at the castle job. Most of them hailed from Melitipol in the Ukraine. They were housed near the showers and those of us working on the castle got to know them pretty well. We regularly used our weekly shower as an opportunity to talk to them in rudimentary German.

Towards the end of winter the air activity started to hot up and the railway marshalling yards at St Veit came in for special attention. At night it was the RAF's turn. The

Pathfinder plane would come over and light up the whole target with target finders called Christmas Trees. We were about four kilometres away and it lit up our area as well. Then the low-level bombers came in one at a time and dropped their bombs. They went home for breakfast and at around 9.00am the American Flying Fortresses arrived, dropping their bombs from about 25,000 feet. If they were lucky they hit the marshalling yards but usually their loads landed in the town or the surrounding fields.

We were regularly pulled out of bed at 2.00am and marched down to the St Veit marshalling yards and made to fill the bomb craters from the night attack. This involved oxycutting any damaged rolling stock, pushing them into the holes, putting ballast on top and laying new rails and points. If the Yanks, by some miracle, landed some bombs on the target we were sent back in the afternoon to repair the damage. We knew how important these repairs were to the German war effort so conspired to work as slowly and inefficiently as possible.

No doubt because of my great expertise, I was transferred back to the pipe-lagging job and it was wonderful to be in the warm again after the bitter cold of the forest. All this time we rejoiced quietly in the knowledge that the war was almost certainly going to finish in 1945. We started to get quite cocky towards Jerry and most of them were prepared to accept our attitude. Air activity was increasing dramatically and there were planes about most of the day and night; fighters patrolled at low level and the bombers cruised away up high. No German planes interfered with them, although we occasionally saw a jet very high up, no doubt reporting on the bomber streams.

Some of the POWs formed relationships with the girls, including me. I was very attracted to Anni Kalugina (later always known as Ann), a high school mathematics teacher before German troops overran her city of Melitopol and closed the schools. Ann was sent to work in a chicken processing factory before ending up with us. Now the girls were doing pick and shovel work while the Russian boys worked on the farm with some of our blokes.

The Germans had by now become quite lax with their security which gave me plenty of opportunities to talk to Ann. When I came down from the roof for lunch or a break, I would often stop and spend some time with her in the courtyard. She was a strikingly attractive woman of medium height with dark, almost black, hair that hung to her shoulders. Sure, there was a mutual attraction but I think that feeling of "being in it together" at a time when our futures hung in the balance really helped to draw us closer. We could both speak reasonable German and our conversations about the war and our respective, but very different, homelands swiftly became more intimate and personal. She was a good-looking, intelligent woman (certainly more intelligent than me) and I was an eager male.

We weren't the only couple. Jack Barker was keen on a girl we called Little Irena. She was a lovely blonde woman but all she wanted was to go home and she didn't want any complications. Cyril Crooks, perhaps not surprisingly, teamed with a rabid Communist girl and they talked endlessly about both going back to Russia together.

As spring approached we knew that this war wouldn't last much longer. No more winters! The British and Americans had crossed the Rhine, were well up into Northern Italy and the Russians were massed on the Oder for the final assault on Berlin. Roll on the Boat! We now started to get our hands on some meat because the Germans had driven all the livestock out of the occupied territories as they retreated. It was welcome addition to our diet because Red Cross parcels had stopped coming, another victim of the Germans' shattered rail system. We didn't, however, have to go down to St Veit to fill in the bomb craters anymore. There was no use repairing the marshalling yards when there were no more trains running.

In mid-April the Russians broke out from the Oder and had only about 50 miles to go to reach Berlin. At the end of the month German news bulletins announced that the Führer has been killed leading his troops against the advancing Russians. It was only later that I learnt he had been skulking deep in an underground bunker under the Reich Chancellery and had committed suicide – a coward's death. The maniac, who had ordered his troops to stand fast and fight to the end, had been responsible for the deaths of millions of people in Europe and Russia. And remember, I still knew nothing of the Holocaust. I think that most ordinary German soldiers didn't know the scale of it either.

Two days before the full surrender, the German Army in Italy threw in the towel and our guards simply opened the gate to the compound and set off for home.

Freedom at last! And what rejoicing! To be fair, our guards had been quite good blokes and we had no ill-feeling towards them at all. We heard that the British were little more than 10 miles away in Klagenfurt so I went to the small telephone exchange and asked the woman operator to put me through to the town hall. She refused at first, saying that for her to do so would be sabotage but eventually I persuaded her to make the call. I managed to reach, I believe, the adjutant of the Coldstream Guards. I asked him what we should do as the Russians were only about 30 miles to the east and we didn't fancy going home via the Soviet Union. He ordered us to stay where we were because they planned to be in St Veit by the next day and would send some trucks to pick us up. He then said that if we were in no danger of being shot then we should disarm any remaining Germans and throw their weapons in the nearest river or lake. We followed his advice and I became the proud owner of a sub-machine gun – a wonderful feeling after four years spent looking down the other end of the barrel.

On the 8th of May 1945, Germany officially surrendered. I had been a POW for one day short of four years. Soon two British trucks arrived. Our blokes were loaded onto one and the Russian women and boys on the other. On the spur of the moment I called out to Ann to ask her whether she wanted to stay with me. "Yes," was the reply before she hopped off the truck. The pair of us, and Lofty, stayed behind in St Georgen for a couple of days before walking into St Veit. I found a room in a house owned by an Austrian woman and told Ann to stay put there until I came back. A battery of the 70th Medium Artillery Regiment had occupied the town so Jack and I reported to the OC. He suggested we stay on for a while to work as interpreters because no one in his unit spoke German. St Veit had become the disarming point for about 200,000 German troops from the southern Russian front. As I could now speak reasonable German I felt I could be of particular help in the disarmament and disposal process.

He wasn't keen on Ann hanging around as his orders were that all Russian nationals must be returned to Soviet lines. However, when I explained that I intended to marry her as soon as possible, he agreed to let her stay as long as she kept out of sight.

The beaten German troops were streaming into St Veit and my job was to direct to where their vehicles, tanks and guns had to be parked in the surrounding fields. Small arms went to another place, and their horses to another. I also arranged German working parties to clear bomb damage and get the town functioning again. One Hauptfeldwebel (Regimental Sergeant Major) was invaluable because he always provided the right number of men at the right time. All German troops had to pass through the processing point where we kept lists of wanted units. These were separated from the run-of-the-mill prisoners and taken to a separate location. Some former SS members tried to slip past by unstitching their distinctive insignias from their collars but they were easy to spot. Any army issue equipment, except for packs and haversacks, had to be handed over but no private possessions were to be taken. The men were then grouped together in batches of 100, depending on their home provinces, and sent off to walk home. Soldiers who had homes which were behind Russian lines had to fend for themselves.

The prisoners had to be moved on quickly because we couldn't possibly feed a couple of a hundred thousand men. The British regiment's headquarters was moved to the town and I struck up a good relationship with the Colonel, who was very helpful to me in the weeks to come. I got some brownie points for making sure the officers' mess was well-supplied with chickens and eggs. My German language skills meant I had become almost indispensable and I had powers far beyond that of a humble Corporal. I took possession of a Kubelwagen (the German Army's equivalent of a jeep) which made getting around so much easier even though I had never driven a car before. Somehow I managed not to hit anybody or anything!

Many Allied POWs were still being rounded up and sent to Italy for repatriation but still left a few roaming around and enjoying their freedom. A couple of real smarties filled the motorcycle side car with Luger and Walther pistols, took them to Klagenfurt airfield and flogged them to the Yank pilots. They then flew the guns to Peninsula Base Headquarters in Naples and sold them at a nice profit. Everybody was happy. It was private enterprise at its best.

One day we received a report that Hermann Goering, a top Nazi and head of the Luftwaffe, was hiding in a farmhouse in northern Austria. I was sent with a patrol to see if we could locate him. After a long drive in two armoured cars we came to the village concerned and made an intensive search. All the locals were questioned but no one knew anything of the Reichmarshall's whereabouts. We returned empty-handed. (Goering had in fact been captured by the Americans on May 9 so perhaps that news hadn't reached our superiors yet.)

Back in St Veit a local informed us that an SS man was hiding in a nearby house. Two soldiers and I searched the house and found him hiding in the bathroom. He was handed to representatives of the Allied Military Government.

The unit then received instructions to investigate a salt mine near St Veit in which it was believed that valuables belonging to Jewish concentration camp victims were stored. Inside the mine we found three large chambers full of people's possessions which had been scattered everywhere. The mine had clearly been looted but the culprits had obviously only been looking for jewelry and valuables. Clothing, fur coats and linen had been trodden into the earth floor. I noted a piano in one chamber and many sets of gold scales, most in velvet boxes. Our informant told us the mine's contents had belonged to Jewish people who had escaped from Austria after the Anschluss. It was heart-rending to see the personal items of so many people treated like this but I took some solace in the fact at least the owners had most likely escaped Hitler's gas chambers. I reported back to headquarters where I was instructed to arrange for a German work party to seal off the mine's entrance.

By now many of the train lines were back up and running. What followed was, to me, one of the most shocking moments of the weeks following the war. Many of the Cossacks who had fought on the German side against the Soviet Union and later surrendered to us were loaded on a train with the Ukrainian girls from St. Georgen and the train left under guard for Unsmarkt – the border between Allied and Russian forces. At Unsmarkt they were all unloaded, taken across the bridge over the River Mur and handed over to the Russians. According to Jack Barker, the men were taken some distance away and machine-gunned to death. The girls were taken down to the river and shot; they were shot like feral animals on the banks of a river in a foreign land. Ann's friend Little Irena was with them – the lovely little girl who only wanted to go home. The shooting of those men, who had fought for the Germans, though very brutal, could perhaps be understood. But, why the girls? They had been wrenched from their homes by the Germans and put to work as slave labourers and had no say in the matter. There is no answer that would satisfy any reasonable human being.

Tito's partisans arrived from Yugoslavia chasing a share of the booty – guns, tanks, trucks, petrol, anything of military use.

There was a real Mexican standoff as the partisans posted a guard wherever we had a guard post. Then they started sitting up in the hills and taking potshots at the Germans on their way home. Eventually we had to arm each group of a 100 German soldiers with 10 rifles and 10 grenades so that they could get clear of the area. In due course a political solution was reached and the partisans departed with a fair share of the loot. I could understand their attitude as they had fought a very long hard war with limited resources.

The CO could now report that all Russian nationals had been repatriated, so Ann was free to move around. We could get about a bit in my vehicle when I wasn't working at the disarmament point but that wasn't very often. I lost it soon after when the order came through that all German vehicles had to be handed in. Ann and I found a little stray dog, a Scotch terrier that behaved quite nervously after being badly traumatised by all the bombing. He scrubbed up quite well after a bath and thrived on a diet of chicken and bully beef.

The town of St Veit was now functioning quite well and the vast majority of the Germans had been moved so my work was virtually finished. The CO told me I would have to be repatriated but that I could take Ann with me. He said we should be able to arrange marriage in Italy. He thanked me for my work and recommended that I be promoted to Sergeant. Then we left our little dog with the woman who had sheltered Ann and were driven down to the airfield at Klagenfurt.

Chapter 13 - Winding Down

CHAPTER 14
HOMEWARD BOUND

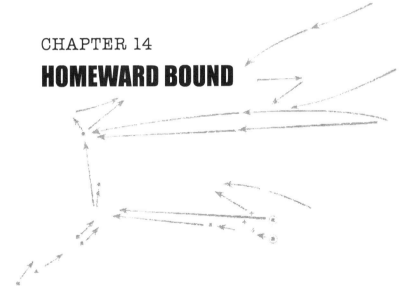

At Klagenfurt we were quartered in a small tent while waiting for the next available plane. After a couple of days we boarded a Dakota with a lot of other odd bods and sods and left German soil for good. For the duration of the short flight we sat on benches arranged along the side of the aircraft. There were no windows which meant I couldn't look down on the conquered land that had held us captive for so long. I wasn't too worried about it. The only thing that concerned me during the flight was the sight of one of the American pilots emerging from the cockpit, plonking himself down and pulling out a Buck Rogers comic. We disembarked at Pomigliano d'Arco airport near Naples. The first thing that struck us at the door of the aircraft was a blast of very hot air. Bella Italia!

We were taken to the small town of Resina (now known as Ercolano) near the city of Naples. Ann was quartered with other women of various nationalities who were waiting to marry British ex-POWs. I was sent to a barracks in the same suburb. Captain Steege was the Australian liaison officer with Peninsular Base Headquarters in Naples and it was he who arranged for us to finally get married. The ceremony took place in Resina's Town Hall with the Captain as the witness.

Needing somewhere to stay we eventually found a room in a house located below Mt Vesuvius. A strong smell of sulphur wafted down from the famous volcano with every rumble or puff of smoke. This was a bit unnerving for me but it didn't seem to worry the locals. It was a unique place to spend a honeymoon. We had two weeks to wait for our flight to England and made the most of it by visiting the Isle of Capri and its famous Blue Grotto, a sea cave on the coast, and checking out Little Vesuvius across the bay from its namesake. The sight of the lava bubbling away, releasing its sulphurous fumes and smoke gave you a good idea what Hades would be like.

I had hung onto a German Walther pistol and a large pair of Zeiss artillery-calibrated field glasses. A bit short of money, I took them down to Base Headquarters and asked the man on the reception counter if anyone wanted to buy them. He went off and found a major and we negotiated a good price. I was a bit sorry about the field glasses but had no regrets about losing the pistol. We were forbidden to take firearms home. Meanwhile, the major could take home his trophies and proudly show them off to his family even though he had never been near the shooting war. Before leaving we had to exchange our Italian lire for English pounds. The official rate of exchange was 100 lire to the pound. However, an English pound was worth 500 lire on the black market and the smarties soon woke up to this windfall. The day before leaving they changed their lire to pounds and then hot-footed it down to Naples to change them back at the black market rate. They then returned to change the lire back to pounds. After repeating that process a couple of times they arrived back in England with a plentiful supply of sterling. I realised later how thick I was because it never occurred to me take advantage of the opportunity.

Naples was very different to a German or Australian city. The narrow streets were crowded with people who had to be constantly on the lookout for the countless White trucks driven by black American servicemen, who seemed determined to break the land speed record. Everybody learned to scatter when they heard them coming. The locals were very friendly and very religious. It was interesting to observe the frequent religious processions through the streets which brought all the traffic, including the White trucks, to a grinding halt.

At last Ann and I were able to board a Dakota bound for England; and this one had seats! A motley crowd joined us, including four nuns, several civilians, some British soldiers and another Australian with his Austrian bride. It was a fine day and my view from the plane's window as we flew over Monaco and France felt out of this world. We landed at an airfield near London and boarded a bus with another group of Australian ex-POWs to be taken to Eastbourne where the Australian Repatriation Depot was located.

Eastbourne was a popular seaside resort but a lot of the guesthouses had been commandeered by the Army. Nevertheless, Ann and I managed to find a room in one of the few guesthouses still operating. All Australian POWs were issued new clothing, paybooks and leave passes. We were officially back in the Army again! On the plus side, my paybook had plenty of money which had gone unspent while I was imprisoned. After four years of a pauper's life everything was good again. Ann and I stayed in Eastbourne for a few days before heading to London to catch the train to Newcastle-on-Tyne where we were to spend some time with my aunt and uncle – headmaster at a local high school – in the suburb of Jesmond. They made us feel very welcome. So, too, did my mother's two nieces – the ones who during the war sent so many prized cigarettes to me … and to Frederick Harvey.

Ann and I quickly fell in love with a sunken park called Jesmond Dene. Virtually in the middle of a very busy part of the city, it was full of beautiful trees, shrubs and flower gardens. You could hardly hear the traffic. We spent quite a lot of time there enjoying the warm early autumn days. Food was still strictly rationed but I had been issued with a good number of ration cards which my aunty gratefully used. One of our blokes bought a small quantity of fruit which came to eleven shillings. He handed the girl shop assistant a pound note and told her: "You had better keep the change. I trod on a grape on the way in". During our stay, sausages came off the rationed list, prompting the joke that it was a good move to free up more sawdust for essential purposes. I couldn't resist buying a slice of watermelon which was very dear.

I had to check in with the Eastbourne depot every few days by telephone and to request another leave pass. However, at the end of October I was ordered to catch the train to London and report to Australian Headquarters in Sloane Square. There I was told I was to immediately catch a bus to Southampton to board the *Aquitania* for repatriation to Australia. Ann was to follow later.

The ship was heaving with servicemen, the majority of them Air Force officers, so all NCOs below the rank of sergeant had to do fatigues (labour of a non-military kind). Confirmation of my promotion to sergeant had not made it through Australian channels so I was assigned to the bakery. It was a good job although it became very hot in the tropics. We started early and usually finished by about 10.00am. If the sea was reasonably calm they would open the large loading door and let the sea breeze in. I had all my meals with the bakers and, believe you me, we ate much better than the rest of the troops. We called at Cape Town and offloaded some South Africans which gave us a lot more room for the rest of the trip. A day's leave was granted but the city failed to impress. We were only too glad to sail east towards the country we had missed so much. We didn't call at Fremantle but stopped in Melbourne before heading to Sydney.

We sailed through Sydney Heads just after sun-up on the last day of November. What a beautiful day it was. The harbour was sparkling in the morning sun and we crowded the rails to point out all the familiar landmarks. It was fascinating to see the ferries again, particularly the Manly Ferry ploughing through that familiar swell as it crossed the Heads. We knew we were truly home when we drank in the marvellous sight of the Sydney Harbour Bridge. We disembarked without much delay and were taken by bus to the Showgrounds where Mum and Mary were waiting for me. I'm not embarrassed to say it was a tearful reunion. "You're much smaller than I thought you'd be," said my mother. Perhaps it was because I was still weighed only nine stone, or maybe she had carried in her mind an image of me as a big, sun-bronzed Anzac hero. Sorry to disappoint you, Mum! That night we stayed with Mary, her husband Merton and son John, before Mum and I caught the train up to Blaxland the following day. I was home at last. And it had been a long way home indeed!

Blaxland hadn't changed much but it seemed a lot smaller. Distances that seemed so great before now appeared to be just a stone's throw. I suppose an adventure which had taken me across oceans and around the globe to North Africa, the Middle East and Europe had given me a little more perspective on where I'd come from. Quite a few of the locals were back from New Guinea and other parts. Jack Ferris, whose family lived next door, was in the 8th Division and had been a prisoner of the Japanese. Jack had been very cruelly treated and was a very bitter man. Thousands of men like him endured a terrible time at the hands of a sadistic enemy. My experience could not be compared, in any way, to theirs.

It was good to see another friend of mine, Don Donaldson. A pilot in an Australian Lancaster squadron, he flew 30 missions in Europe and was awarded the Distinguished Flying Cross.

It was also wonderful to breathe that fresh Australian mountain air again and to know, after six years of an enormous struggle, that everybody was free once more and ordinary life could start again. Thankfully, my mother had managed quite well during the war with my allotment and her war widow's pension. More importantly, she owned her own home and had no rent to pay. Later my sister told me that mum's darkest moments had been in the long period between being advised that I was wounded and missing until it was confirmed I was a POW.

Chapter 14 - Homeward Bound

CHAPTER 15
INTO A DIFFERENT WORLD

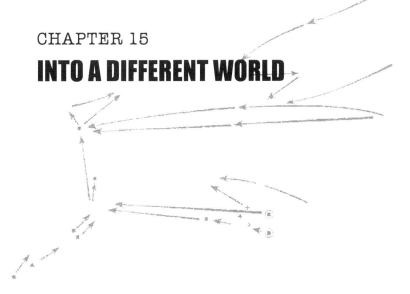

I was discharged from the army in late January 1946. A couple of weeks later I returned to my old firm, Major Bros. I thought their initial salary offer was a bit light on but that was quickly upped to six pounds a week. Nine years had passed since I started work in their city office in 1937. I thought it was a good idea to get back to work as quickly as possible. Some blokes spent quite some time knocking around after the war and then found it hard to settle down.

I was drawn to the company of the men I had come to know so well during the war and I was lucky to catch up with some of them who, because of their length of service, were already back from New Guinea. Gary Hart, Mac Wilson and Brian Waring, all privates in the early days, were now lieutenants and Mac had ended up in command of the signal platoon. I had very few fond memories of POW food. The only thing I missed was the heavy potato flour bread which sustained us for so long. Even the local brown bread seemed to have no substance. It wasn't until continental bread came onto the market quite a few years later that my craving was satisfied.

In the meantime, Ann was in England being looked after by my aunt and uncle in Newcastle while she waited for a ship to Australia. In late March 1946 I received an air mail letter to say she was leaving on the *Rangitata* and would arrive in Sydney in about five weeks. After such a long separation I was really looking forward to us being together. My job was going well and I had settled fairly easily back into civilian life. Anzac Day 1946 was a terrific highlight of the year. After the march through Sydney we held our reunion in upstairs premises near Wynyard station. What a day it was! Many original members of our platoon converged from all over NSW and it was wonderful to see them again. Beer flowed freely and there were many "do you remembers?".

I was living with Mum at Blaxland while my sister and her husband were building a new home at Strathfield. When Ann arrived the plan was to move into my sister's current house and take over the tenancy when she moved to the new one. I thought it was a good idea to hire a car for a couple of weeks to show Ann around but I still had no licence. I picked up the car and drove to the testing station at the back of the Sydney Hospital. The policeman who tested me remarked that I clearly hadn't done a lot of driving but he gave me my licence and some parting words: "Good luck". There were no "L" or "P" plates in those days.

Ann's ship docked in Melbourne and she caught the train to Sydney. It's hard to describe the joy I felt when I saw her step off that train. Fortunately, her trip out had been a happy one. She'd met a lot of fellow war brides who we kept in contact with for a few years afterwards. I proudly helped Ann into the car and off we set off for Concord where my family was waiting to welcome her. Her English had improved dramatically but there was still the occasional stumble, like the time she spotted a sign in Burwood that read: "Tasty Snacks". She was horrified because she thought it said "tasty snakes".

Ann settled well into life in Australia and we were very happy together. For a while I drove a small used Austin, but it couldn't pull the skin off a rice pudding so I traded it in for a Flying Standard 14 coupe. On my first Christmas holidays we drove up to Teven, near Lismore, to visit a fellow former POW and his Russian wife on their dairy farm. Our happy life was complete when our daughter, Sandra, was born in 1948, and blighted only by the sad death of my mother shortly after. She was a wise, kind and gentle woman who taught me so much.

I still have a letter from her dated April 3, 1942, and this excerpt reveals a lot about her:

"Dear Charlie. I hope you are well and that you will be home soon. In the meantime I know you will make the very best of things. I remember reading a book Mr. Scorer sent you when we were at the flats and I quote:

'To think rightly is to create
All things come through desire
We become like that on which our hearts are fixed
Keep your mind on the splendid things you would like to do
Then you will find the opportunities that are required for
the fulfillment of your desire.'
Dear Charlie it is a perfect day in Blaxland and although it is April the weather is still warm."

That letter was written five days before my first escape from Groppenstein. Sorry, Mum, the desire was certainly there but I was a bit lacking in the fulfillment!

Towards the end of 1948 the Citizen Military Force was reformed and I rejoined the 30th Battalion as the signal sergeant. It had no shortage of recruits and in short time was at good strength. In 1949 I was commissioned and became platoon commander. In 1952 I was promoted to captain and later became Officer Commanding HQ Company, which I had originally joined as a cadet in 1938. My life had come full circle.

Chapter 15 - Into A Different World

CHAPTER 16
REFLECTIONS

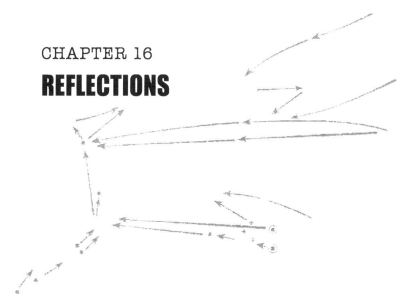

One of the few virtues of old age is that one can look back on the past in an objective way, free from the passions and prejudice of youth, and seek to find the truth even though this may, at times, be difficult and sometimes distasteful.

Memories of my very young life are nothing but pleasant. The Depression left me unmarked. I was too young to feel its grinding poverty and living on a farm meant it always seemed as if we had food. I realise now the importance of having very good and stable parents. And mine were just that.

Life in an infantry battalion is a powerful experience. The battalion becomes your family and remains so for the rest of your life. I write this with the knowledge that it's likely only three of the 34 men of my platoon, which came together in 1939, are still alive. I sincerely hope our loose cannon, Snowy Downs, with whom we have lost contact, might be out there somewhere. Rusty McWilliam, Bruce Cork and I have kept in regular contact for more than 63 years.

The platoon had some marvellous reunions, usually on Anzac Day, but watching our numbers dwindle over the years has been sad. But even that can never diminish the amazing feeling of belonging that we experienced during the war. That is what being part of an infantry battalion does to you!

Religion, that great divider of the human race, did not affect our relationships in any way. Your fellow soldier's religious beliefs were never important when you huddled together in a slit trench. It was more so when you were POWs. The intense training in Palestine welded us into a unit and made us very fit. But it also gave us the opportunity to meet people of other nationalities and backgrounds – the British soldier, the Palestine policeman, the Jews and the Arabs. All this was quite a culture shock for Australians used to living in isolation at the other end of the world, but it served to broaden our outlooks.

We were blooded in the Western Desert campaign against an inferior enemy but his bullets and shells could still kill. It was hard-going in the desert, but there was one big plus; there were no civilians to become casualties of war. We advanced rapidly and there is no doubt that being part of a victorious army was quite exhilarating, particularly when casualties were comparatively light. Unfortunately, all we gained was very quickly lost when the Germans came on the scene; all except for Tobruk, where Rommel learnt just how well the Australian soldier could fight. Boy, did they teach him a lesson.

To withdraw a battle-hardened division like the 6th Australian and send it to Greece to carry out an impossible task seemed to be a dreadful blunder. However, Greece was our only ally in that theatre of war, so attempting to help them was probably the honourable thing to do. But, to be honest, perhaps the only thing we accomplished was dragging the Germans down into Greece with no chance in the wide world of stopping them.

Greece to us was a magical place after the deserts of Palestine and Libya. Camping under the pine trees near a little wandering stream was something to savour. Particularly memorable for me was the one day's leave in Athens when we sat at tables on the pavement outside the hotel in Omonia Square and drank with friendly locals. Although they were mostly women and old men, this was something new to us. The young men of Greece were busy thrashing the Italians in Albania. There were some very attractive girls about but taking one out was not exactly a joy. She had to be accompanied by an adult chaperone and with only one day's leave this left very little room for manoeuvre. Nevertheless, Athens was a lovely and warm city and what happened under the German occupation, when Greeks died from starvation on their own streets, was tragic. It was one of the many stains on the character of the German people.

The size and might of the German Army was quite a shock to us. However, the Australian and New Zealand divisions gave a very good account of themselves in the Anzacs' first encounter with the Germans in Europe. The battle at the Monastir Gap is still to receive the attention it deserves from historians, but it's worth noting that three battalions held their positions against one of the finest divisions in the German Army – Leibstandarte SS Adolf Hitler – for the best part of four days and suffered heavy casualties in the process. The cold and snow was alien to us, whereas the enemy had white smocks which made his troops hard to pick out. Luck was with me at Brallos Pass, as it often was. To have a bracket of four big shells land all around you and sustain only one wound was mind-boggling. The downside of that stroke of luck was that it separated me from my battalion and ultimately resulted in me becoming a POW. My most abiding memory of Greece was the beauty of its countryside and the courage and compassion of its people.

Where do they lie, those young men who perished in the sands of the desert or in the snows and olive groves of Greece? Their warrior souls have long left for their personal Valhalla. They live only in memories of those who knew and loved them. But their countries must always remember them, for they paid the ultimate price for the wonderful postwar period we have enjoyed since our powerful enemies were denied their victories.

Many years later I visited the serene war cemetery at Phaleron, near Athens, where some of the men of my battalion who died in the fighting in April 1941 now lie alongside many others. It is a lovingly-tended cemetery with a bed of flowers in front of every headstone. At the entrance of the cemetery the names of the fallen, grouped by battalions or units, can be found on big marble plinths.

Life in captivity was a mixed bag and most of it has been detailed but the interesting thing was trying to work out the German people. It is difficult to comprehend how the majority of intelligent human beings could allow themselves to be so utterly dominated by one man. The SA and the SS quickly made sure that the minority learnt the error of their ways. Everybody from paper boy to the general ran around giving the Nazi "Heil Hitler" salute with right arm outstretched. We wondered what it would be like if all Australians went around saying "Heil Menzies". I have a feeling the salute would have involved the middle digit pointing skywards.

Our biggest ally in the European war was Hitler. As Supreme Commander he led his armies from disaster to disaster, and eventually to destruction. He was responsible for the murder of millions of Jews and others in one of the worst genocides in history. If ever a war was just it was World War II. Our way of life would have vanished if Germany and Japan won.

The German soldier was a good soldier. In my experience they usually behaved correctly to us. However, being part of such a system sometimes required them to carry out orders they knew to be morally wrong. A German soldier had to swear an oath of allegiance to the Führer. When they asked us why we kept trying to escape, we always replied: "It is our duty as a soldier." They accepted this because of their strong sense of "deinst" or duty.

We had enough to eat, apart from the period of captivity in Greece and that wretched train trip. Red Cross parcels helped us remain relatively healthy and although the winters were harsh we avoided the diseases that ravaged those poor blokes in Japanese hands. There were no obese POWs. Our cholesterol count was probably pretty close to zero; although in those days we didn't even know what that was. My strongest memories of German food involve potatoes, potato bread and mangel-wurzel soup. Mangel-wurzel is a root vegetable mainly grown as stock feed but I doubt that any self-respecting cow in Australia would eat it. To be on the inside of a conquered country was a unique experience. To see a strong country with a powerful army crumble around you was to sense victory in the extreme.

After the war Germany and Austria were full of people of all nationalities; men, women and children who had been forcibly brought in from virtually every country in Europe and Russia. Most were trying to get home. All were trying to get food and shelter. East Germans were torn between the desire to go home and their awful fear of the Russians. There was a political agreement between the Soviet Union and the Western powers that all Russian nationals must be returned to them. Almost two million Russians had died in captivity but more than a million were sent back. Most were sent to Gulags in Siberia; many were shot. There is no logical reason for this vile behavior. Perhaps the only possible explanation is that Stalin didn't want anyone who had been exposed to Western ideas. Or perhaps it was paranoia? Who knows? In fact, the only things those poor old Russians had been exposed to was starvation and cruelty. All they wanted was to go home. So much for Communism!

A POW learns very quickly that only four things matter for survival: food, water, shelter and clothing. The absence of one of these essentials makes life very precarious. Even with all four, a POW feels as if he only exists as he fights or waits for freedom. One thing shines like a beacon through the gloom in such circumstances and that is mateship. It provides the strength to battle on and survive till the sun shines again. To all my old mates, most of whom have since left this earth, a sincere thank you. I think of you often with reverence. Friendships formed in adversity are deep, pure and unaffected in any way by rank, possessions, outsiders or religion. They can rarely be replicated in the materialistic consumer society we live in today. I believe such friendships need real adversity to flourish, or perhaps I am too pessimistic.

My most powerful memories involve the mateship of the many men with whom I shared the war. They are nearly all dead but I see them not as old men, but as the almost knightly figures of their youth – strong, earthy and totally reliable. There are history books that describe the campaigns in the Western Desert and Greece but not much out there covers comprehensively the four years many of us spent as POWs. I had only one man to consult in my efforts to make this book as accurate as possible and that was my old mate Jack "Lofty" Barker in New Zealand. As far as I know all the rest are dead. Jack is 88 and has a remarkable memory of those places and events so many years ago. I phoned him often in the course of writing this book and he always came up with the answers. Bless you, Jack.

As prisoners we knew there were concentration camps – a small one was located near to Leoben – but were completely unaware of Germany's extermination camps. I strongly believe that the average German and the average German soldier didn't know either. The enormity of the Holocaust was fully revealed after the war and exposed a side of the German character we had not seen. The map on page 111 shows the locations of these camps in the Third Reich and Poland. The extermination camps were all located in Poland out of sight of the German homeland. If Germany had won the war, its people would have been deluded into thinking they were squeaky clean.

The change in the German people as the war progressed was quite noticeable. It seemed to me in 1941 that virtually every German I met believed Adolf Hitler was his country's saviour. Most worshipped him. Before Stalingrad they had complete confidence in his leadership even as their cities were being destroyed by Allied bombs. The doubters appeared after Rommel's defeat at El Alamein and the loss of the 6th Army at Stalingrad. Fear made them very careful about voicing their concerns but talking to a POW was pretty safe; he wouldn't put them into the Gestapo.

After the D-Day invasion of Normandy, the irresistible advance of the Russian armies towards the German border and the increased bombing of their cities, the doubters didn't doubt anymore. They knew Germany would soon be "kaput". This doubt spread to the soldiers, too, but their discipline and fear of the Russians made them fight on when victory was clearly impossible. After D-Day, Field Marshal Gerd von Runstedt, Commander-in-Chief on the Western Front, told German Supreme Headquarters: "Make peace, you idiots!" But Hitler would have none of that. Hundreds of thousands of soldiers and civilians died unnecessarily in the last weeks of the war as he insisted on fighting to the end. Then he sneaked out of it all by killing himself.

Ann and I had some good years after the war but she had very high emotional needs which I failed to meet. She was a remarkable woman but suffered some 20 years of severe physical and mental illness until her death. This was a very difficult time, particularly for our daughter, but she showed great strength of character to come through it. Those years caused me great remorse but Persian scholar Omar Khayyam had it right when he wrote:

"The Moving Finger writes, and having writ,
Moves on: nor all your Piety nor Wit
Shall lure it back to cancel half a line,
Nor all your tears wash out a Word of it."

I have since remarried and Wendy has brought a bright light into my life. A few years ago we made a pilgrimage back to that magical land of Greece. It's a country that is very familiar to my daughter, Sandra, who is the Classics Mistress at one of Sydney's largest colleges. She said: "Tell them, Dad, that you are Australian and they will do anything for you." And, boy, was she right! We had a wonderful cruise around the Greek islands and over to Turkey, but unfortunately couldn't get to Spetses. On our return we visited Lamia, Brallos Pass, Megara, Corinth and Nafplion.

The woods of Daphni were almost as beautiful as the day I first saw them. Wendy, who is an accomplished artist, painted a beautiful picture. Today it hangs in our home as a constant reminder of those days during my long journey 67 years ago.

Canberra, 1998 – old mates,
Charles Granquist, Joe Wishart
B.E.M. and Ernie Wolfe,
back together again.

The guns are silent now,

The dove of peace is on the wing again,

Battlefields are 'neath the plough,

*And the voices of the millions whose dues
were paid, are but faintly heard.*

Only we very few can hear them clearly still.

We beg of you, don't let it happen ever again.

"LEST WE FORGET"

Charles Granquist

ABOUT THE AUTHOR

Charles Granquist was born in 1922, at Blaxland in the Blue Mountains. His father served with the A.I.F. in World War I and was wounded in France in 1917. When war broke out in 1939, Charles increased his age to 19 and joined the A.I.F. sailing with the 2/4th Battalion on board the *Strathnaver* to Egypt.

Charles served with his battalion in Bardia, Tobruk, Derna and Benghazi before being wounded in Greece in 1941 and captured by the Germans. Charles then experienced life as a Prisoner of War and was incarcerated in a number of different European prison camps, including Markt Pongau, Feldkirchen, Wolfsberg and St. Georgen, as he went through an amazing journey of escape, recapture and punishment.

After six years serving overseas, Charles returned to the Blue Mountains where his Russian War bride, Ann, later joined him. Charles had a successful management career and later joined the Citizen Military Force, was commissioned and his life came full circle when he became Officer Commanding HQ Company. Charles now lives with his second wife, Wendy, in the coastal town of Port Macquarie in New South Wales.